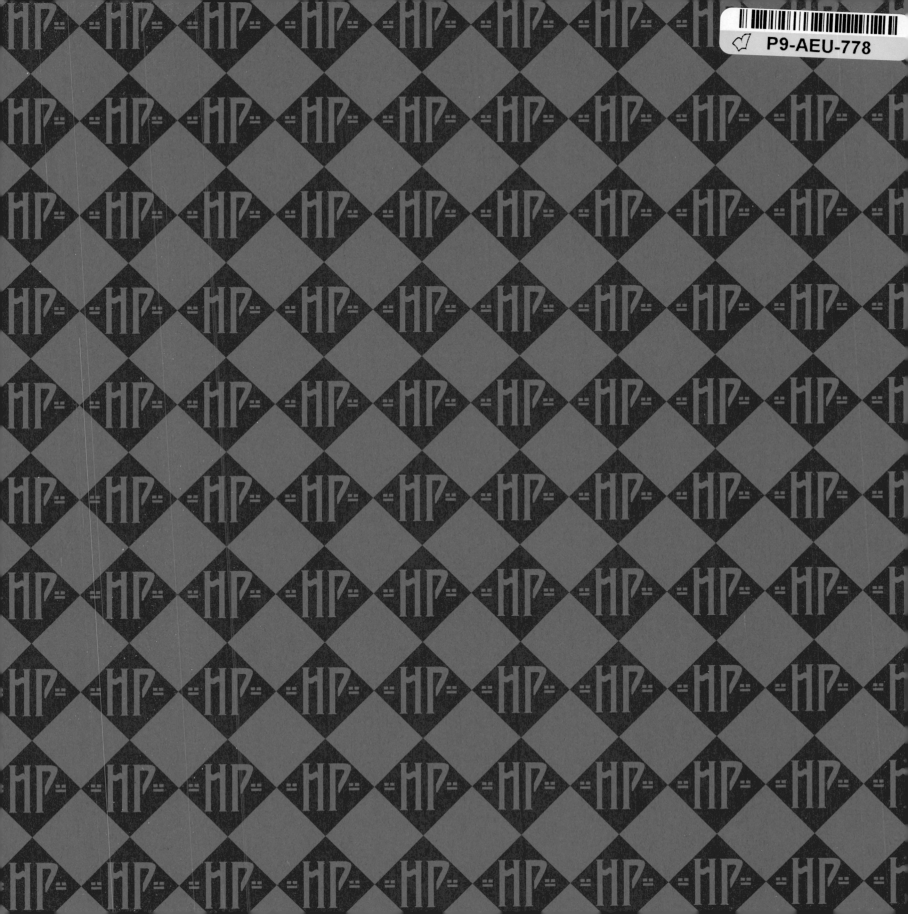
P9-AEU-778

*"When you drink from the well,
remember the well-digger."*

Chinese Proverb

Inside the Hotel Pattee

Lela Gilbert

Photography Bill Geddes

PINATUBO
PRESS

© 2004 Pinatubo Press
Copyright to the original artwork remains
in the name of artist who created it.

All rights reserved. No part of this book
may be reproduced or transmitted in
any form or by any means, electronic
or mechanical, including photocopying,
recording, or by any information storage
system, without written permission of
the publisher.

RAGBRAI® is a registered trademark
of The Des Moines Register and Tribune
Company. Used under license. All rights
reserved.

Inside the Hotel Pattee
Text by Lela Gilbert
Photography by Bill Geddes
ISBN: 0-9742683-0-5
Library of Congress Control Number:
2003110274

Project Manager: Ann Hirou

Book Design: ReynoldsWulf Inc.
Robert M. Reynolds, Letha Gibbs Wulf
and Brett Reynolds

Additional photography: Ellen Bak
Robert M. Reynolds

Copy Editor: Chris Moore

Printing/Pre-Press: Printing Today

Bindery: Roswell Bookbinding

Floor Plan Illustrations: Martin Milward

Printed and bound in the United States
of America

Table of Contents

Preface

When our company purchased the Hotel Pattee in September of 1993, I wasn't sure just what we were going to do with it. Over the next year, it became clear that this building, so much a part of the history and fabric of the life of Perry, Iowa, needed to tell the town's story. The building itself would become the storyteller, its rooms the pages of a complex and compelling tale.

Perry was largely settled by immigrants from Sweden, Germany, Ireland, some from Italy, and Bohemia, what is now the Czech Republic. The town's early history included struggles with language and culture. Other immigrants came through the years, from Cuba, Vietnam, Laos, Somalia, and Sudan. The Latins who came in the 1990s were the largest group to arrive in some time. Given the turmoil of the world, it seemed to me that small towns where people who differ — religiously, ethnically — yet learn to trust one another have a special story to tell. And that story could be told, in part, in the hotel.

Underlying all the sagas of the people who came to settle the Midwest was the magnet that drew them in the first place. That magnet is the land — rich, dark, fertile soil, a farmer's dream. All the public spaces of the hotel are named for the land, two for specific soils found around Perry — Nicollet and Canisteo. In those rooms, the visitor may even see core samples of the soils themselves.

Rising from the land was the heritage of the wide variety of buildings these settlers erected. William and Harry Pattee, the original builders of the Hotel Pattee, had dreamed of a grand hotel, a place that would make Perry the talk of the region.

Their vision propelled them to Chicago to select a design. For the exterior they chose Federal Style, a type of architecture popular across the country for more than forty years after the centennial of the United States in 1876. But for the interior they were inspired by one of the public rooms of the La Salle Hotel, a room done in English Arts and Crafts Style. That style is rooted in the notion that the craftsman and woman are to be honored, that materials are to be natural and used so as to honor nature. In keeping with that vision inspired by William Morris, the visitor sees interiors shaped by wood and stone, tile and woven fabric, patterns from nature, such as birds and leaves, vines and trees. In everything there is the unmistakable hand of the craftsman or woman who fashioned it in the first place. Some of the rooms and the public spaces directly reflect the work of some of the greatest architects and designers in that tradition — William Morris and Gustav Stickley in the lobby, meeting rooms, library, and ballroom; Charles and Henry Greene of California in the board room; and Frank Lloyd Wright in the lounge.

Not only did the rooms need to tell the story of the immigrants and their encounter with the land, but they also had to celebrate the people and history of the Midwest. Consequently, along with the Irish, Mexican, Dutch, and other ethnic rooms, there are the Chautauqua, Alton School, Angus and Moran, and other rooms that tell the history of a place or a movement with roots in Perry. Beyond that, though, the rooms celebrate individuals, such as Betty Mae Harris, known for bringing dance to Perry children for thirty seven years, or V.T.

"Snick" Hamlin, the Perry boy who created Alley Oop, or Louis Armstrong, the jazz great who had the good grace to stay at the Hotel Pattee.

As you look around, let the beauty of art speak to your soul. Throughout the hotel are more than 100 pieces of original art, much of it commissioned for the hotel. Pieces in the public spaces were chosen intentionally to conjure the beauty of the land and its people. In the rooms, art was selected to tell the particular story of that room. In the William Morris Room, for example, all the furniture was commissioned from a contemporary English Arts and Crafts furniture maker. Using a kit specially created by England's Royal School of Needlework, a group of area embroiderers recreated Morris's famous Red House daisy hangings for the draperies. All the fabrics are Morris designs.

Finally, the hotel had to tell the story of the Milwaukee Railroad, the town's largest employer for more than 100 years. To do that, David's Milwaukee Diner welcomes the guest through a railroad car door into the ambiance of a 1913 train depot complete with the sign from the old depot in Perry.

In many ways, the hotel is an album full of pictures and stories. We invite you now to open the cover, turn the pages, and share the magic and the meaning of one small town set on the Prairie but connected to the world.

Roberta Green Ahmanson
10 November 2003

Right: International flags welcome guests to the Hotel Pattee.

An Invitation

Those who travel extensively come to take both landscape and lodging seriously. They find pleasure in exploring well-known scenery, from whitewashed seaside inns to snow-clad mountain peaks and rustic cabins. Observant travelers also appreciate the subtle beauty of less well-trodden vistas — the country lane, farm fields crowned by weathered barns, and the patchwork of small towns.

Take Iowa, for example. Travelers who cross America "from sea to shining sea" may well find their way to Iowa, whose name, according to some Indian traditions, means "the beautiful land." Beautiful, yes, although Iowa's beauty can be difficult to describe. James Hearst writes,

No one who lives here
knows how to tell the stranger
what it's like, the land.
I mean the farms all gently rolling,
squared off by roads and fences,
creased by streams, stubbled with groves,
a land unformed by the mountains' height
or tides of either ocean,
a land in its working clothes....
its muscles bulge and swell in horizons
of corn, lakes of purple alfalfa
a land drunk on spring promises,
half-crazed with growth — I can no more
tell the secrets of its dark depths
than I can count the bushels
in a farmer's eye as he plants his corn.

Settlers began to populate Iowa during the westward movement of the early Nineteenth Century. Indian tribes — the Ioway, who gave the state their name, along with others — were gradually displaced and moved further west, while farmers developed their homesteads, and railroaders laid gleaming tracks across the plains. Before long miners were searching for coal, teachers were establishing schools, merchants and craftsmen were launching their businesses, and people of faith were building churches.

Perry, Iowa, about thirty-five miles northwest of Des Moines, became an important railroad town as well as an agricultural center. By the turn of the Twentieth Century, Perry was thriving, its populace made up of various ethnic groups bonded in a community by shared experiences: working the land, cherishing family life, practicing faith, providing education, and surviving losses. In the midst of these experiences, one quality emerged that brought Midwestern towns like Perry to life: Vision. That vision — the gift of imagination — was revealed in such diverse media as needlework and quilting, visual arts, musical performance, dance, cartooning, and perhaps above all else, an entrepreneurial spirit.

At the heart of Perry, Iowa, is the Hotel Pattee. Originally built by two enterprising brothers, Harry and William Pattee, the hotel opened in May 1913. Over the years its fortunes mirrored the community's, fluctuating with the Iowa economy. Pattee Enterprises Inc. purchased the Hotel Pattee in September 1993, and Howard and Roberta Green Ahmanson became its patrons. By then the hotel, along with Perry itself, had fallen on hard times.

Roberta Green Ahmanson is a native daughter of Perry, and like many who love Iowa, she longed to "tell the stranger what it's like, the land...." She grew up in the expansive prairie landscape, among Iowa's thoughtful, practical, and well-read people. She had learned as a young girl the values of hospitality and of fellowship around hearty meals. The Hotel Pattee was an integral part of her past, and she saw it as an important key to Perry, Iowa's future, a place where visitors could encounter a careful combination of collective memory and comfortable lodging.

In Mrs. Ahmanson's words, "I knew that if the hotel deteriorated any further than it had already, it would be the last straw to downtown Perry because it was such a big building. If it ended up being demolished, it would take the heart and soul out of the town. I didn't want to see that happen. So I thought, I can fix this up. And that's how it all started."

Fix it up she did. But she did much more than that. She brought together architects, interior designers, woodworkers, artists, and artisans skilled in an array of media. Temporarily closed for renovation in 1995, the hotel reopened on May 29, 1997 — eighty-four years to the day of its first opening. The invited guests at the Grand Opening Dinner witnessed a transformation.

Roberta Green Ahmanson had been committed to retaining the integrity of the original hotel's Arts and Crafts motif. And that was only the beginning. Each of the forty guest rooms is designed and decorated differently, each one focusing on a culture or nationality,

Left: John Preston, *Late Summer Morning,* 1997, Oil on canvas, 35 x 47.5 inches

a trade, a noteworthy person, or a local hero whose past has intersected Perry's.

It is almost impossible to enjoy the comfort and beauty of the guest rooms without realizing that there is a specific significance to every detail — from lamps, to pillows, to fabrics, to furniture, to fine art. Nothing has been done by chance. Working closely with Mrs. Ahmanson were her lifetime friend, Pam Jenkins, who is also a Perry native and a sociologist who studies communities, and interior designer Tracie McCloskey. Their research; faithfulness to time, place, and style; and creative energy have resulted in a unique marriage of sophisticated design and historical narrative.

The colorful pattern of small-town stories is woven into the fabric of Midwestern America. The rooms of the Hotel Pattee, like interactive museums, recount people, places, and things, each one a strand in a larger tapestry. Hotel public areas and guest rooms alike pay tribute to the way of life that has animated Midwestern life for two centuries. And the more than 130 pieces of original art in the Hotel, rendered by more than thirty artists, reflect the vision that continues to enliven the community.

Since reopening, the Hotel Pattee has received numerous awards, including AAA's coveted Four Diamonds. It was named the Iowa Lodging Association's Property of the Year in 2002, and Iowa Attraction of the Year in 1999. Its restaurant, David's Milwaukee Diner, earned *Wine Spectator* magazine's coveted Award of Excellence in 2001, 2002, and 2003, under the direction of executive chef David North.

R.W. Apple, Jr. of *The New York Times* has written that the Hotel Pattee is "…a magnificently restored Arts and Crafts gem that few American towns could hope to match…."

Meanwhile, travel writers, too, came to see for themselves. *Nordic Reach* magazine, for example, wrote, "The Ahmansons' renovation has completely restored the hotel's neoclassical exterior and arts and crafts interior. More importantly, it has restored something to a declining community: pride and belief in a future for small-town America."

In California, the *Orange County Register's* travel writer Gary Warner declared the Hotel Pattee his favorite United States hotel. He explained, "One of the joys of traveling is that even after years on the road, I can still be surprised. This year the surprise was this hotel on the plains northwest of Des Moines. I knew the Hotel Pattee was…a gem beloved by Arts and Crafts enthusiasts. But I wasn't ready for the sense of artistic whimsy that inhabits every room…."

A guest's first impression of the Hotel Pattee hospitality is often a crackling fire and a warm welcome. But guests rarely have the opportunity to see every guest room — the rooms are usually filled with other visitors. Since there are few things Roberta Ahmanson enjoys more than taking special guests on a private tour of the restored hotel, a "virtual" viewing is in order. As you read the pages that follow, you will not only explore and discover every corner of the hotel, you will also hear the thoughts of Pam Jenkins, Tracie

Roberta Green Ahmanson

McCloskey, and others who have contributed to the Hotel's renaissance. And you will hear about some favorite memories, seeing the rooms of the Hotel Pattee through the eyes of Roberta Green Ahmanson.

Left: The Challenger Dining Room.

Except the Lord buil[d]
they labour

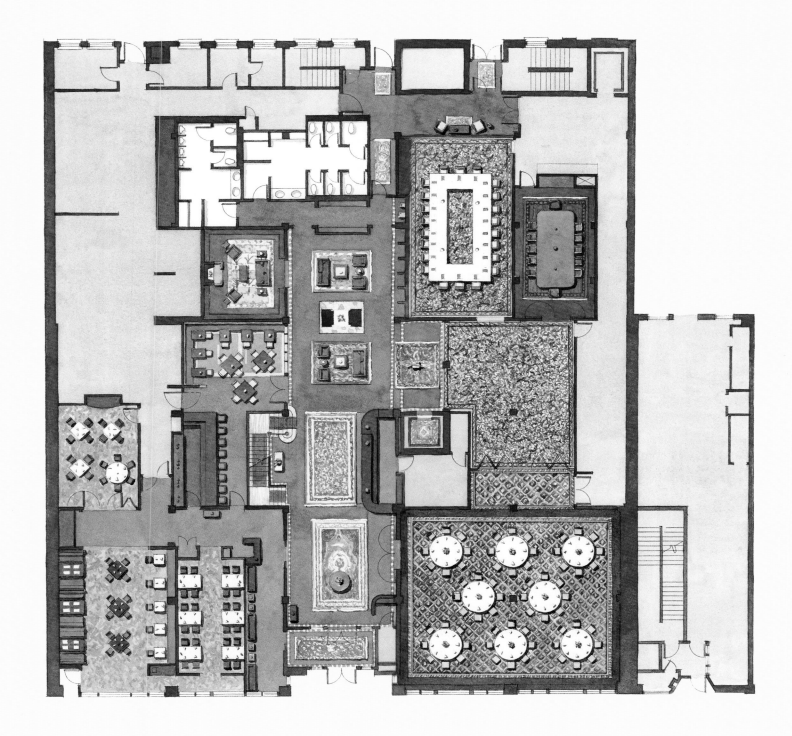

Welcome to the Hotel Pattee

International flags snap smartly in the wind as your car pulls up in front of the Hotel Pattee's facade. The doors swing open and you are greeted by a friendly doorman, dressed in 1913 style, evoking the Hotel's earliest days. Your eyes scan the lobby and, if you're like most people, you catch your breath. You take a moment to enjoy the mahogany paneling, the fresh flowers, and the Persian rugs that stretch across the terra cotta floor, leading to an immense stone fireplace.

After a quick look around, you move to the reception desk at your right. Just behind it is "Mother and Child," a painting by Gary Ernest Smith whose work is prominently displayed throughout the Hotel. A woman stands in front of her orange-red barn holding her child, smiling broadly. Like everything around her, she too seems to be wholeheartedly welcoming you to what one reporter has called "the most surprising hotel in America."

Every detail of today's Hotel Pattee was carefully envisioned, planned, and implemented, and Roberta Green Ahmanson believes that its restoration and hospitality represent two important aspects of her life's calling. On the lobby's back wall is an inscription from Psalms 127:1, "Except the Lord build the house, they labor in vain that built it." Mrs. Ahmanson explains its significance to the restoration of the community landmark.

"I call it one of the two pillars, or two bookends, of the hotel — bookends that hold together the stories of the hotel. It is there because I firmly believe that unless every enterprise we engage in is connected to the Author and Giver of life, that enterprise will die. It will surely fail. And that goes for the Hotel Pattee.

"The other pillar, or bookend, is on the wall of the Spring Valley Ballroom, just around the corner from the lobby. The Chinese proverb says, 'When you drink from the well, remember the well-digger.'

"I learned that proverb from Caroline Ahmanson, my husband's stepmother. And it's really what the hotel is all about — it's about remembering the well-diggers. Perry, Iowa, and the Pattee brothers had no idea that Roberta Green would ever be born, let alone that she would eventually have a hand in the renovation of the Hotel Pattee. Nevertheless, what I've done is to stand on their shoulders, on their effort, and on their vision. People whose faces we will never see and whose names we will never know have made decisions that impact our lives greatly."

In the process of reconstructing the Hotel, the lobby was modeled as much as possible after the original. "So that if Harry and William Pattee walked in," Roberta Ahmanson explains, "they'd say, 'Yes, I remember this place.' We wanted to keep the Arts and Crafts notion, so we got Stickley reproduction furniture. There are two couches, four chairs, and a table — all Stickley. Their leather cushions are in keeping with the original lobby."

Opposite: The Hotel Pattee Lobby, 2003
Below: The Hotel Pattee Lobby, 1913

Spring Valley Ballroom

Before taking the elevator up to your guest room, curiosity will probably get the best of you. If so, you'll want to take a few minutes to visit some of the public areas on the Hotel's ground floor. Your first stop, directly behind the registration desk, is the Spring Valley Ballroom, which is named for Spring Valley Township — one of sixteen townships in Dallas County, Iowa.

Along with the second "bookend" — the proverb that Mrs. Ahmanson has described which is imprinted on the frieze — there is a mural titled "Spirit of Perry" by Doug Shelton, colorfully chronicling the history of the town.

On its left side, the mural recounts the construction of the railroad in the late Nineteenth Century — it was the railroad industry that first established Perry as a viable community. Artist Doug Shelton describes his work:

"Beginning with the far left scene, we see an Ioway Indian sitting on a woven reed mat. He is seeking a vision, which appears in the sky. In the clouds is the shape of a train, symbolizing the changes that are about to come to his world and the vehicle that will implement them. He has painted himself with red earth, has a bear claw necklace and a wolf tail hanging from his hair roach. This late summer scene takes place at dusk, foreshadowing the end of his way of life. At the time of this scene (pre-European contact), wolves and bears, including the occasional grizzly, lived in the central Iowa region."

Next, toward the center of the mural, are reproductions of newspaper stories about the town — St. Patrick's Church, the old fire station, the Jones Building, a marching band, and the high school newspaper. Then the artist moves the viewer into another time and place, where a train hurtles along its now-completed tracks, corn pushes upward, promising a bountiful harvest, Louis Armstrong performs a trumpet serenade beneath a full moon, and the Ringling Brothers, Barnum and Bailey Circus comes to town.

Doug Shelton concludes, "I love painting large. The scale was very exciting and painting large is a physical activity; you're standing on ladders, sitting on the floor, and moving around a lot. Painting techniques can be a bit looser and yet will still read well. It takes a lot of energy. Doing the research is always interesting. It is never too late to learn something new."

These images of Perry — painted large — represent the efforts of a few of the many well-diggers who first established Perry. They planted the town's roots deep into the Iowa soil where it remains to this day. In Roberta Ahmanson's view, they must not be forgotten.

But the Spring Valley Ballroom is more than just a place for remembering the past. Today it has once again become, along with the Hotel Pattee's fine restaurant and lounge, a focal point in the life of Perry.

Left: Spring Valley Ballroom with mural (Doug Shelton, *Spirit of Perry*) *Right:* Mural detail.

Dallas County Boardroom

Leave the ballroom and step through the lobby extension pre-event area, where there are photographs of Howard F. Ahmanson, Jr., Roberta Green Ahmanson's husband, and his father. Pass another Gary Ernest Smith painting, "Celebration of Life," which depicts a fiddler offering a musical blessing to a freshly tilled field, and enter the Dallas County Board Room, named for Perry's home county.

Here is a California connection. A hand-fashioned table and chandelier designed and crafted by James Ipekjian, a California woodworker who specializes in Arts and Crafts interiors, are the central focus of the room. Of the inspiration for his work, Mr. Ipekjian says, "One hundred and ten years ago Charles and Henry Greene established an architecture practice and went on to create some of the most distinctive native structures the United States has ever seen. Drawing on the vocabulary the Greenes used — Asian design motifs coupled with Scandinavian woodworking techniques — I attempted to create a conference table and chandelier that would not only respect the work of the Greenes, but also would be mindful of the multiethnic history of Perry, Iowa."

James Ipekjian fashioned the table of South American mahogany and ebony, with a modeled floral inlay design of curly koa, bloodwood, pink ivory, snakewood, mother of pearl, and copper. The elongated oval shape is an adaptation of a *tsuba*, or Japanese sword guard; the

"If we do not know the past, we are condemned to repeat it."
— George Santayana

flowers his interpretation of a simple trailing rose. The table is surrounded by Eames chairs and crowned at either end with an "Egg Chair" designed by Arne Jacobsen. The chandelier and ceiling plate are also made from South American mahogany, ebony, and brass with iridised art glass assembled using the copper foil technique.

On either side of the table, two large pastels by Iowa artist Bobbie McKibbin are prominently displayed. Of these works Mrs. Ahmanson says, "One is a red painted corn crib out in the country somewhere — it's so Iowa. On the other wall is a marvelous pastel of the Alton School, which was on the outskirts of Perry. Students went to school there for nearly 100 years. The

community moved the old school through town to Forest Park Museum, and it's there today — completely intact. The painting was made of the schoolhouse in early winter, snow-covered, seen through the reeds. It's marvelous and evocative."

The work of James Ipekjian and the pastels of Bobbie McKibbin combine the West Coast interpretation of the Arts and Crafts Movement with the images of the land and life of the Midwest.

Left: Dallas County Boardroom *Above:* Bobbie McKibbin, *Red Corn Crib Summer*, 1997, pastel on paper, 40 x 64 inches

Canisteo Room

Next door is the Canisteo Room, a middle-sized meeting room. The room is named "Canisteo" after a type of Iowa soil. "Not the finest soil," Mrs. Ahmanson remarks, "but a very good one." On the room's back wall is a sample of Canisteo soil provided by Iowa State University, located in Ames, Iowa, about thirty-five miles from Perry.

On one side of the room are pastels created in 1997 by Ellen Wagener, who has spent much of her artistic career portraying Iowa field scenes. Her three pieces form a triptych titled, "Landscape — Suite in Three Movements." On the opposite wall is a large collection of vintage photos. Roberta Ahmanson explains, "I wanted to have photographs of the families that had been the industrial foundation of Perry and also of important buildings in Perry. So we have displayed photographs along with postcards of the churches. There are photographs and pictures of H.O. Wiese, and the H.O. Wiese Company, as well as Osmundson Manufacturing Company and the Bruce family, who are the people behind Osmundson. Along with industrial photographs, there are also pictures of Perry founder Harvey Willis, the Willis family, businesses, and the Carnegie Library across the street from the Hotel Pattee. There's an informal history of Perry in photographs on that wall."

Left: Canisteo Room with historic photographs.
Below: Ellen Wagener, *Landscape: Suite in Three Movements,* (one of three images), 1997, pastel on paper, 38.5 x 57.75 inches.
Bottom: Historic photo of Willis Avenue.

Willis Library

By now, your guest room is beckoning you to unpack and relax a little before dinner. But one more stop is essential. The Willis Library offers a wonderful collection of classic videos and books — very important elements in your evening's relaxation. Outside the library is a picture of Ned Willis, his son David, and David's son Jeffrey, all of whom were present at the Hotel opening. Descendants of Perry founder Harvey Willis lived in Perry until Ned Willis died in 1998. During the time of the Hotel's renovation, Ned Willis served as an advisor.

Roberta Ahmanson: "This was quite appropriate because all the Willises I ever knew read a lot of books. David Willis was a compatriot of mine as a kid. We grew up together. We were in journalism class together, and he's been a friend ever since high school. The library was intended to be a place where people who stayed in the hotel could come and get books and videos. There's a classic video collection. There is a collection of features from the Biography Channel and a lot of videos about the themes in the hotel. There are also a few contemporary movies."

Hotel Pattee guests can also receive an honorary library card at the Perry Public Library, across the street from the hotel, and rent books or videos there. Mrs. Ahmanson says of the Willis Library, "We have attempted to provide things that you would not necessarily get at the local library. The Hotel Pattee's library books are related to themes in the hotel."

In the Willis Library are more Gary Ernest Smith paintings. There is also a group of "Humpties" by Perry folk artist Betsy Peterson. Her whimsical creations are seated on shelves among the books and the videos, happily reading. The library is furnished with Stickley furniture and is warmed by a wood-burning fireplace featuring a hammered copper hearth-cover. Copper is a favored material in Arts and Crafts interior design, and Mrs. Ahmanson thought the library was the best place to feature it. Not a few guests find it difficult to make up their minds as to which book would be most informative or which video would be most entertaining. It is helpful to know, while a decision about an evening's diversions is being made, that hot coffee or cold drinks can be served in the gracious ambiance of the Willis Library.

Left: Willis Library with painting (Gary Ernest Smith, *Autumn Harvest*). *Above:* Jeffrey, Ned, and David Willis. *Right:* Copper fireplace hood detail.

Inter-Urban Lounge

Whether the occasion is a drink before dinner, a quick visit with a friend, or an informal afternoon card game, if you're in Perry, Iowa, the Inter-Urban Lounge at the Hotel Pattee is the place to go. And one glance inside tells you that you're in no ordinary hotel bar. Complemented by the interior design of Tracie McCloskey, architect John Leusink created the lounge in the manner of Frank Lloyd Wright, the consummate Midwestern Arts and Crafts designer, the signature person of the Prairie Style.

Frank Lloyd Wright's influence is evident in every aspect of the Inter-Urban Lounge's design. All the seating in the lounge is reproduced from original Frank Lloyd Wright designs. The stonework was inspired by a photograph of the Herbert Jacobs residence in Madison, Wisconsin — an example of Wright's Usonian Design. The back bar shelving was inspired by Wright's Fallingwater — the Kaufmann Residence in Western Pennsylvania. The pole lamps are reproduction Wright, as is the stunning chandelier. The original chandelier, called the Butterfly, is in the Dana Thomas House in Springfield, Illinois.

The walls are fashioned of stretched fabric panels, which were created by Sean Brown, an Iowa craftsman. Of his technique, Brown writes, "The one-foot by one-foot wall panels were inspired by a picture of Frank Lloyd Wright's Brown House, explicitly the linear tile pattern over the fireplace. These panels

were cut on a computer-controlled cutter to obtain completely square panels. The panes were wrapped with fabric and then installed onto the walls. The large fabric panels were tightly stretched on a track system. The fabric pieces under the bar next to the rock were quite time consuming, being cut from a Micore panel and pushed and glued into place."

Sepia-tone photographs of Perry's history, and particularly of the Inter-Urban Railroad, are informally displayed in the lounge, along with a wall of photographs chronicling important events in the history of the hotel and the town.

Of the lounge, architect John Luesink says, "Frank Lloyd Wright's ideas transformed architectural thought. He challenged conventions. He loved architecture, perhaps, above all else. The Inter-Urban Lounge's intent is to provide a sample of his palette of materials and spatial design. It was our wish that this place not only be a pleasant environment in which to relax, but also

to explore the creativity of one of our greatest American architects."

Left: Inter-Urban Lounge. *Above:* Historic photo of Carnegie Library Building and Hotel Pattee. *Below:* Inter-Urban Lounge with historic photographs.

David's Milwaukee Diner

Dinner at the Hotel Pattee is a special occasion, in large part because of the fine culinary accomplishments of Chef David North. The menu at David's Milwaukee Diner, which changes daily, boasts the finest contemporary cuisine based on the bounty of an Iowa harvest. To achieve this, Chef North has built relationships with the Iowa Practical Farmers, a group that produces organic foods such as lettuce, asparagus, strawberries and sweet corn, as well as organically-raised chickens and, as the Practical Farmers say, "Chevre cheese fresh from our local goat Tillie." The combination of Chef North's creative recipes, local produce acquisition, unforgettable desserts, and an exceptional wine collection make for an extraordinary dining experience.

But, as everyone knows, a great dining experience has everything to do with its setting. And the restaurant, like the rest of the Hotel Pattee, has a few stories of its own. David's Milwaukee Diner is divided into three separate dining areas, each displaying fine art and a unique ambiance.

"The concept behind David's Milwaukee Diner," Roberta Ahmanson explains, "was that it would resemble a railroad depot restaurant of the highest quality. At the beginning of the 1900s those places were done in a kind of Arts and Crafts way, with wood paneling and booths. David's Milwaukee Diner looks a lot like that. You enter through a railroad car door that you push and it

slides open like the door on a railroad car. As you enter and hang up your coat, you'll see a collection of old photographs of the Milwaukee Railroad—the people that worked on the railroad, pictures of trains, and other memorabilia. You'll see a sign that says 'Perry, Iowa' that was taken off a railroad crossing on Second Street, and it is kind of priceless. In the entryway is another sign that was originally from the railroad superintendent's building before it was torn down, citing the 'Perry Division.' There's also a big 'X' that says 'Railway Crossing.'"

The first room to the left, called The Arrow, is design to look like a railroad dining car. The Arrow was once the "milk train" that stopped at Perry, which means that it stopped at every other station, too. The color paintings in the Arrow dining room represent windows,

as if the viewer were a train passenger looking out across the Des Moines River Valley. The paintings are impressionistic, rendered in watercolor by Woodward, Iowa, artist Dennis Adams.

The main dining area is called The Challenger. The wooden booths and the banquette feature carved leather railroad scenes by Des Moines artist Will Ghormley. Of Ghormley's work, Roberta Ahmanson says, "There are nine panels in the restaurant, all historic scenes of the railroad out on the prairie somewhere. One is the story of Iowa's Kate Shelley, who became a national

Left: Challenger Dining Room at David's Milwaukee Diner with mural (Doug Shelton, *The Hiawatha*) and carved leather panels (Will Ghormley). *Below:* Train door to David's Milwaukee Diner.

The guests are met, the feast is set, May'st hea

heroine when she climbed across a damaged railroad bridge in a storm, averted a railway disaster, and saved the lives of hundreds of passengers. Will Ghormley won the American Institute of Architects Award for the best use of an unusual material in an architectural setting. He sculpted leather to make the panels and then painted them. The results are just incredible."

Above the tables and booths in The Challenger are two murals, painted in acrylic on canvas by artist Doug Shelton. One is called "The Hiawatha." Shelton writes, "The mural shows the Milwaukee Railroad's Midwest Hiawatha pulling out of the Perry station heading east to Chicago sometime in the early 1930s. The streamlined and polished Hiawatha was a stunning example of mid Twentieth Century passenger train design. In 1933, when it was first introduced, it set a record speed of 112.5 miles per hour. On the left is a 1937 Ford, another masterpiece of art-deco design. People are milling about, watching the train depart or heading to their destinations."

On the opposite wall is Shelton's mural, "The Perry Train Station, Early 1900s." Doug Shelton describes the scene. "This mural shows the hustle and bustle of the station with the arrival of the Chicago, Milwaukee, and St. Paul's engine number 520, a coal burner. It is a 4-4-0, which refers to the wheel arrangement from front to back. As was typical of the time, the first car after the coal tender was the mail car. I painted the mural with the idea of it being a play; the train is the backdrop and each individual an actor. I'll leave the story up to the viewer."

The third dining area in David's Milwaukee Diner is the Hiawatha, and it features paintings by Fairfield, Iowa, artist John Preston, representing the four seasons. Preston chose separate Iowa locales, one for each season. "The winter one is a place southwest of Perry," he says, "and the other three are from Johnson, Danbury, and Jefferson counties. They are places I go by on a regular basis and I see them all year round. Some of them I've painted six or seven times in different types of weather and different seasons."

Roberta Ahmanson describes her conversation with Preston regarding the oil-on-canvas paintings. "He said he had always wanted to do the seasons, but he wanted them to be displayed together. When we gave him the commission for four paintings, it was his opportunity and indeed they are together. So if you dine in the Hiawatha Room and look at the Four Seasons in Iowa, you get to see how close spring and summer are. It's hard to tell the difference if you don't read the names of the paintings. There a difference but it's subtle. You have to look for it."

Left: The Hiawatha Room at David's Milwaukee Diner. *Below:* Historic train photo. *Next:* East light court with sculpture (Karen Strohbeen and Bill Luchsinger, *Animals, Flowers, and Stars*).

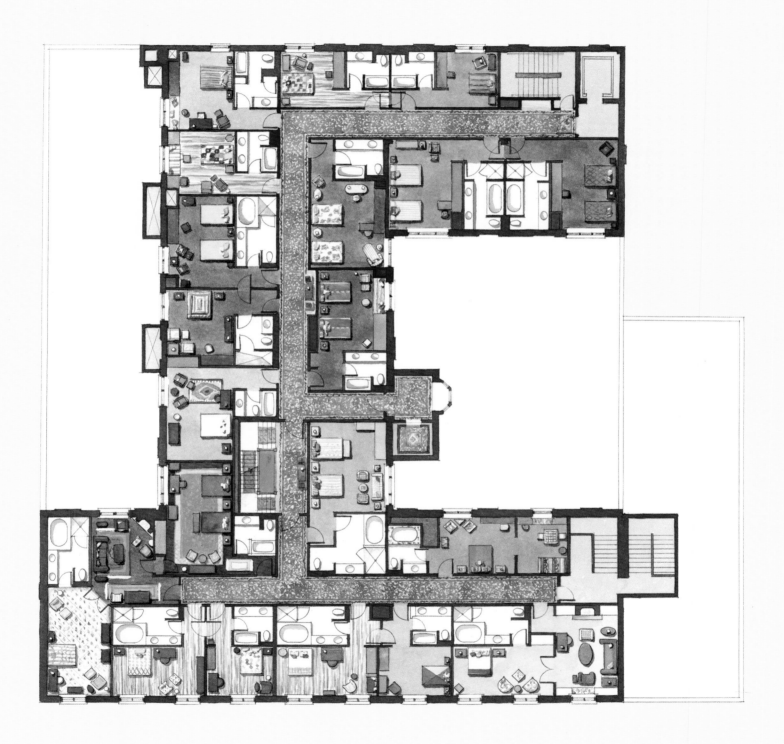

Earl and Virginia Green Suite

Delight thyself in the Lord, and he shall give thee the desires of thine heart. – Psalm 37:4

The story of Perry, Iowa, is the story of hard-working settlers, many of them emigrants from other lands, people who were devoted to their families, cherished their faith, sought after quality education, and exhibited the strength of character to survive their losses. The Green Suite in the Hotel Pattee embodies that story, honoring two Perry townspeople who are very dear to the heart of Roberta Green Ahmanson. It is named for her parents, Virginia Olson and Earl Green.

Virginia and Earl, like many of Perry's residents, were of Swedish stock, although in Earl's case, his Swedish mother married an Irishman. As we will see, the Swedish community in Perry was large, influential, and strong in faith. Roberta Green grew up in a devoutly Baptist home. Swedes, particularly, were not only pious but were very involved in the railroad industry. Virginia Olson Green's father and grandfather worked for the railroad, and when Earl Green left the Coast Guard, he too went to work for the Milwaukee Railroad, where he served as an engineer until he retired in 1978.

There are four large suites in the Hotel Pattee, each with a wood-burning fireplace. As she contemplated remodeling the hotel, Roberta Ahmanson decided early on that one of those suites would honor her parents. Once that decision was made, thoughts about decorating came quickly. "I didn't even have to think what the decor would be because my father had built the house at 1623 West Third and Paul Streets," Roberta recalls. "My parents had just moved into it before my birth. So when I was born, in 1949, that's the house I went home to.

"My father did all the design for the house and chose the decor. The exterior was painted white, and it had a green-and-white striped awning. There were green shutters on some of the front windows. Inside, the living room and dining room were forest green and all the woodwork was white. On one wall my father built shelves where my mother kept her bell collection."

Today the Green Suite reflects the home Earl Green designed and decorated for his family half a century ago. There you'll see Wisconsin artist Steven Kozar's watercolor paintings, which offer images of the homes the Greens lived in for over forty years. "Waiting for Grandma" is particularly poignant as it depicts the Green home during the 1950s. Virginia Green's bell collections are now on display at the hotel, one group at Christmas, the other during the balance of the year, just as they always were in the Green household.

Reflecting the popular colonial style of the American 1950s, the furniture in the Green Suite is maple, accented with colorful chintz fabrics, braided rugs, doilies, and ballerina lampshades. A white chenille bedspread completes the familiar surroundings, along with family pictures, such as a photograph of Earl Green serving on a Coast Guard boat, and another of Virginia Olson as a little Iowa girl.

Earl Green died in 1991, so he never visited the suite that is named in his honor. He was a source of strength and encouragement to all who knew him, and his loss continues to be keenly felt. But his words of wit and wisdom live on, including "Never Let the Honeymoon End," along with one of Virginia Green's favorite scriptures, Psalm 37:4, all of which are stenciled on the Green Suite frieze.

Today, Virginia Olson Green has moved away from Iowa and lives in Southern California near her daughter, son-in-law, and grandson. But when the opportunity arises, she is always delighted to return to her hometown and to stay in the Hotel Pattee where she feels very much at home in the Green Suite, sharing the latest news with her beloved Perry friends.

Above left: Earl and Virginia Green. *Below:* Part of bell collection.

David Ahmanson Suite for Kids

Traveling with children is inevitably an adventure, and parents who take their offspring along on holiday soon learn to expect the unexpected. For such courageous explorers, nothing could be more unexpected — and more cheering — than the Kids' Suite at the Hotel Pattee. Designed by Sticks®, a Des Moines firm that specializes in functional art, the suite is sophisticated enough to appeal to adults, while capturing a child's imagination. There is a king-size bed for parents and bunk beds for kids. And for the sake of travelers of any age who deserve a special treat, the Kids' Suite comes complete with cookies and milk at bedtime.

Sticks' unusual approach, Roberta Ahmanson says, "…is kind of a contemporary version of Arts and Crafts if you will, combining art and usefulness." Sticks' designers, Sarah Grant-Hutchison and Jim Lueders, have developed a unique style of design, much of which incorporates the use of found tree limbs, branches, or twigs into its form; hence the name "Sticks®."

There are many creative elements interwoven into the Sticks' Kids' Suite installation at the Hotel Pattee, but two are immediately apparent. One is an explosion of color — high-energy

shades of purple, green, yellow, and red — providing an almost irresistible mood lifter.

The other element is a collection of proverbs, which are painted throughout the rooms. When Sarah Grant-Hutchison first discussed the Kids' Suite with Roberta Ahmanson, she says, "I thought, wouldn't this be a nice way to teach life's lessons? So I covered all the walls with proverbs from all over — Biblical proverbs, ancient Chinese, whatever, with little pictures to go with them. What a great way to learn!"

The official title of the guest room is "The David Ahmanson Suite for Kids," so named because, at the time of the Hotel Pattee's development, the Ahmansons' son David was almost six years old. Although other bathrooms in the hotel are fitted with black and white tiles, everyone decided to take a more colorful approach in the Kids' Suite, so the tile company gave a pattern to David and asked him to fill in the colors. He selected turquoise, yellow, and red. All the framed art in the room is David's, too, created during first, second, and third grades.

A huge, stuffed blue lizard shares the Kids' Suite with guests, as does a wooden

tooth fairy sculpture, attired in a pink and silver frock, magic wand and all. And for those who are interested in playing chess while enjoying their milk and cookies, there is a game table, equipped with Sticks' kaleidoscopic vision of knights and bishops, kings, queens, and pawns, all fashioned of brightly painted wood.

Above left: Sticks® lamp finial. *Left:* Drawing by six-year-old David Ahmanson. *Above right:* Kids' Suite detail with Sticks® bunk beds and game table.

R.M. Harvey Room

When the circus first came to Perry, Iowa, in the late Nineteenth Century, the news traveled quickly around town and rippled out across the prairie to the homesteads and farms in the surrounding area. And it wasn't just the little children who got excited about this spellbinding new kind of local entertainment. With the arrival of Kirkhart's Wagon Shows in 1894, *Perry Chief* co-publisher R.M. Harvey caught circus fever too, and soon he was involved with national advertising for the three-ring event. Before long he was working for the circus itself as a contractor. Eventually he became affiliated with the Ringling Brothers, Barnum and Bailey Circus. His love for the circus and his flair for advertising brought business to Perry that contributed to the community's commercial success for decades.

Harvey spent most of his ninety years associated with the great names of the circus world. He died in 1959, and the late Ned Willis was executor of his will. "There was a time," Willis said, "when half of the circus posters in the United States were printed in Perry, Iowa." This was because while R.M. Harvey was a partner with the Ringling Brothers Circus, he was also serving as part owner of the *Perry Chief*, so the circus posters were printed at the *Chief's* printing plant in Perry.

The R.M. Harvey Room's decor recalls the glory days of the traveling circus with its bright triangles of primary color, antique posters featuring Kit Carson and Hoot Gibson, and a miniature red and white circus tent partially canopying the bed. Many of the photographs and the circus memorabilia that decorate the room's walls came to the hotel through the generosity of R.M. Harvey's nephew, R. Lynn Johnson, who lives in Des Moines. Artist Alice L. Porter carved the two miniature carousel animals, which have been fashioned into bedside lamps. Ms. Porter lives in Ogden, Iowa, only fifteen miles from Perry.

"What's interesting about R.M. Harvey," Pam Jenkins says, "is that he's an example of a small-town guy with a big idea. He took that big idea and turned it into the circus business, which he and others operated for a long time out of Perry. Many of the hotel rooms are a reflection of a man or a woman with a big idea and enough energy and creativity to make it work."

Above left: R.M. Harvey
Below: Carousel horse by Alice L. Porter

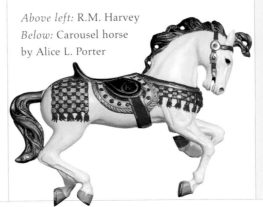

Alice L. Porter
Ogden, Iowa

Woodcarver Alice L. Porter grew up in Perry, Iowa, during the 1940s and 1950s, and enjoyed many childhood celebrations at the Hotel Pattee, where she also took dancing lessons from Betty Mae Harris. She carved the carousel pieces for the R.M. Harvey Room from basswood, also called Linden wood, which is native to Iowa. "Mr. Harvey's contribution to our community was laughter, bright lights, music, and the childlike joy brought by the circus. For his room I was asked to try to bring some of that circus joy to life in a pair of bedside lamps — a carousel horse and a menagerie lion.... Since figures on a carousel are supposed to engage our imaginations, bring us joy, and are not supposed to frighten anyone, the animals are carved with gentle faces and non-threatening poses. The horse is a queen's horse with gold-leaf mane and tail. The lion carries a cupid on his shoulder and is meant to express the strength and beauty of love. Neither animal is frightening and children could have ridden them off into their fantasy world of princes, dragons, and beautiful damsels in distress."

Barry Kemp Room

*S*mall Town Boy (or Girl) Makes Good: besides being the plot line of a thousand novels and almost as many movies, it is a recurring theme at the Hotel Pattee. For Barry Kemp, it is a continuing, real-life story. And as that story pertains to the Hotel Pattee, there are some very important things to remember. One, Barry Kemp spent two years, give or take, in a small town called Perry, Iowa. Two, he translated that experience into some very amusing and successful television and movie productions. Three, Barry Kemp has been gracious enough to allow the Hotel to name a room after him and to donate memorabilia to complete the room's decor. And that's because, even though Barry Kemp became very successful in the entertainment business, he never forgot the people in Perry he knew as a young man.

Like R.M. Harvey, Barry Kemp had the kind of special gifts — vision and imagination — that, along with hard work, can carry a gifted person a very long way in the world. A talented and astute writer, Kemp's work reflects the people and places he's observed in the course of his life. Along with "Newhart" and "Coach," Kemp helped create "Taxi," a more urban drama, but still mirroring the insights of a man who has taken enough time and maintained enough interest to understand ordinary people's personalities, behavior, and humor. Barry Kemp also produced several movies such as "Romy and Michele's High School Reunion" with Lisa Kudrow and Mira Sorvino, "Patch Adams" with Robin Williams, and most recently "Catch Me If You Can" with Tom Hanks and Leonardo Di Caprio.

Barry Kemp went to Perry High School with Pam Jenkins and Roberta Ahmanson. "In Sociology, we have a term called the sociological imagination, created by C. Wright Mills. It is how a person's own biography is related to history, " Pam Jenkins says, "Even though he wasn't born and raised in Perry, Barry Kemp really remembers the time he spent in the community, and that history is reflected in 'Newhart' and in 'Coach.'"

In the spring of 1996, when the renovation of the Hotel Pattee was under way, Roberta Ahmanson wrote to Barry Kemp, "We're naming some of the rooms after people who came from Perry and did something in the world, and I want to name a room after you."

Kemp's response was to the point, "Sure, you can do it, and I'll help you in any way I can." He provided posters, a jersey from "Coach" and a jacket from "Newhart," mugs and photographs and scripts. Football helmets from Coach were made into lamps.

At Barry Kemp's request, designer Tracie McCloskey used the set of "Newhart" as a model for the decor. Paneling was installed similar to that on the set; the same style of Windsor chairs were selected, and fabrics were all in keeping with the time frame of the show. Even a hand-hammered iron chandelier was duplicated.

Of course Roberta Ahmanson wanted to make sure that she invited Barry Kemp to be the first guest in the Barry Kemp Room. And since he would be in town anyway, did he mind saying a few words?

"Well, this far in advance I can't say no," he replied. "I'll come."

"He packed out the room," she recalls with a smile. "He spoke at the opening. And it was lovely."

Above left: Barry Kemp (third from left) on set of the pilot episode of *"A Minute with Stan Hooper." Below:* Barry Kemp alcove with football jersey from *Coach.*

Cream 'n' Eggs Room

Sometimes, as we've seen, the fulfillment of a local person's "Big Idea" brings a portion of fame and good fortune to the community. During our tour of the Hotel Pattee, we'll revisit this theme again and again. But at other times, the "Big Idea" was less glorious and far more necessary. During such difficult times as the Great Depression, as Roberta Ahmanson puts it, "A lot of farm women sold cream and eggs from the farm to provide the money that meant the difference between starvation and non-starvation. It was money that made their lives survivable….When I asked Pam Jenkins for suggestions for room names, she suggested that there should be a room named Cream 'n' Eggs, for those women who held their families together selling cream and eggs from the farms."

In Midwestern farm communities, women customarily brought cream and eggs to town on Saturday to exchange for money or goods. Although this was an especially important enterprise during the 1930s, it continued for decades.

The Cream 'n' Eggs Room at the Hotel Pattee honors the women who toiled alongside their farmer-husbands, making the most of the soil, the animals, and the marketplace.

Of her interviews with elderly farmwomen, Pam Jenkins says, "I have heard great stories. When a town girl married a country boy, for example, and she moved out into the country, often as a wedding present she was given 300 baby chicks. Well, these town girls, even though they are from small towns, didn't know the first thing about chickens. And some of them weren't successful and said, 'Oh, my chickens all died from the heat,' or 'My chickens all died from the cold.' But they had to learn. Because when you couldn't get money for crops and you couldn't get money for your cattle, you could always get money for cream and eggs. During the Depression, especially all through farm life, these women provided a constant source of cash for farm families. And so they were really, really important and often unacknowledged."

To walk into the Cream 'n' Eggs Room is to walk into another world. The carpet was woven to represent the homemade rag rugs that cover the floors of many an Iowa home. All around are the cheerful colors and practical artifacts of the early Twentieth Century. A collection of milk bottles and an old churn recall the cream; a rooster weather vane the eggs. On the ceiling above the bed is a Murray Johnston art quilt, "The Old Barn Door." But the most evocative display of all may be the two women's dresses, carefully framed, which are fashioned of feed sacks, a recycled fabric

women often used to clothe themselves and their children when every penny counted. In the days of Cream 'n' Eggs, self-indulgence was unheard of, and the "Big Idea" was the most important idea of all: making sure the family's needs were met.

Above left: Feed sack dresses. *Above:* Murray Johnston, *The Old Barn Door*, 2000, quilt, 36 x 44 inches. *Below:* Chicken weathervane.

1913 Farmhouse Room

Closely related to the Cream 'n' Eggs Room is the 1913 Farmhouse Room, which also depicts life on a Midwestern farm. Both rooms take a reflective look at days gone by, without forgetting that life on the farm was never easy.

Pam Jenkins, who has interviewed dozens of farmers and their wives, describes their way of life. "In the early days of farming you had cattle, sheep, pigs, goats, ducks, chickens, and you grew the crops for your animals. People were attached to their animals. One farmer I interviewed said 'I love my cattle.' He still has a few cattle that he keeps for sentimental reasons. Today farmers keep a few cattle or they might keep some pigs, but again, farming has changed. Now the focus is on crops, not animals. But the Farmhouse Room is about that old kind of farming where people worked from sunup to sundown almost every day, summer, winter, all year."

On the walls are sepia-toned photographs of a typical farm in the first decades of the Twentieth Century, depicting the hard work that went on there. A cow weathervane reminds us of the farmers' love-hate relationship with the weather. And on one wall are kitchen implements, including old dishtowels and an apron. A quilt by Janet Pitman, patterned with chickens and chicken-wire shapes, hangs behind the bed, once again recalling the contributions made by both farmers and their wives toward supporting the family and building the communities that make up the heartland of America.

Above left: Antique sewing machine.
Above right: Threshing Machine, c. 1920.
Right: Kids on horse on Purviance Farm, south of Perry, c. 1910. *Below right:* Fabric scrap ball.

D.J. Pattee Suite

Whether you lived on a farm or a house in town, May 29, 1913, was a night to remember in Perry, Iowa. Here's how the *Perry Chief* reported the evening's events:

"The opening of Hotel Pattee last evening was without doubt the largest event of its kind ever held in Perry. Hundreds of Perry people and friends of Perry from outside the city participated in the magnificent banquet…and in the festivities which marked the opening of the most complete and sumptuous hostelry in the state of Iowa."

Henry and William Pattee — whose success in both the grocery business and banking was well known in Perry and throughout the Des Moines area — built the Hotel Pattee to honor their father, early Perry settler David Jackson Pattee. They constructed it with a style and grandeur that seemed appropriate to their family's success story.

A brochure from the hotel's early days features a photograph of one of the rooms with a four-poster bed, decorated in the Victorian style, even though the Hotel Pattee's finished architectural interiors were Arts and Crafts. Today's Pattee Suite was planned with this early room in mind. Its colors are warm-toned, its furniture of rich wood, and its details typical of an elegant suite of rooms in the early 1900s. With a fire glowing in the fireplace, surrounded by vintage artifacts, it is easy to imagine being a guest in the first incarnation of the hotel. In fact, a portion of the floor in the Pattee Suite is actually a remnant of the original Hotel Pattee.

Roberta Ahmanson explains, "We couldn't save much of the wood from the floors of the old hotel because it would just crumble in your hands. But the original hotel had a café on the second floor that had a wood floor, and some of that floor was not in bad shape, so we saved a good portion of it. That wood is the floor in the living room of the Pattee Suite — the one place where there is original hotel wood on the floor."

Photographs of the Pattee family are displayed in the suite. Jean Pattee McDonald, who was eighty-six years old when the Hotel restoration was complete, contacted Roberta Ahmanson after reading about the renovation of the Hotel. She is the daughter of one of the two original builders of the hotel, and she and her daughter, Susan Snedeker, were the first two guests in the Pattee Suite when the Hotel Pattee reopened in 1997. Many of the pictures now on display in the suite are from her personal collection.

Above left: D.J. Pattee, c. 1912.
Above: D.J. Pattee Suite bedroom.

Swedish Room

BLOTT ÄR DET SOM EVIGT ÄR UNGT ·

Half a world away from Perry, Iowa, set amidst Sweden's northern forests, the province called Dalarna is an area rich in folk customs and traditional celebrations. Local towns are represented by *dala hestes* — folk horses carved of wood with a long tradition that can be traced back hundreds of years. In fact, the Dala horses have become a folk symbol of Sweden. Each town had its own symbolic horse.

Also in the Dalarna region is a little town called Sundborn, site of one of Sweden's most famous homes, the home of artists and designers Carl and Karin Larsson. Larsson memorialized both the life and design of that home in dozens of paintings and drawings, eventually putting them in a book called *Ett Hem* – "At Home." The Larsson vision, connected to the Arts and Crafts movement in Scandinavia, continues to influence design to this day. In fact, the Larssons revived a style currently in vogue in America – Gustavian style, named for the taste of an Eighteenth Century Swedish king.

Swedish immigrants flooded into America in the mid-1840s. Many were farmers headed to Wisconsin, Minnesota, Illinois, and Iowa. By 1910, 1.4 million Swedish — first- and second-generation immigrants — were resident in the United States while, at the same time, the population of Sweden was 5.5 million. There were enough Swedish people in Perry for a part of the town in its early days to be called "Swede Town." So Roberta Ahmanson, with her own Swedish roots, decided early on that there would be a Swedish room in the Hotel.

"On my father's side," she says, "the immigrants were Emma Sjöstrom and her husband, John Fluborg, who must have left Sweden in 1878 or '79. They came to Perry in 1880. My grandmother said that they stopped in Perry because it was 'the last safe place for women and children' off the railroad before you went further west."

Roberta's maternal Swedish great grandparents didn't come to America together. They met on the boat en route and married in 1889. Her grandfather was born in 1890 in Clive, Iowa. He was a railroader, like his father, who had been the foreman of the crews that repaired the track. In 1932, her grandfather was transferred to Perry, where he was the chief night dispatcher. His name was Arthur Oscar Olson.

Considering all this, of course there would be a Swedish Room. But what would it look like? After Roberta Ahmanson's first trip to Sundborn, the die was cast. "I told myself, I'm going to do Arts and Crafts in this hotel. And if this is the Swedish room, then let's take the people who kind of epitomized a very special piece of this from Sweden. So we decided to replicate the style of Carl and Karin Larsson."

Architect Ernie Adams was commissioned to create the room's interior. Tracie McCloskey researched every aspect of the Swedish Gustavian style, from beds to chairs to tables, and incorporated it into the room, which contains some authentic Gustavian furniture.

Sean Brown, a craftsman from Radcliffe, Iowa, fashioned the wainscot, base, cap, and window valance in the Swedish Room. Of his work he says, "The most challenging piece was the handmade archway over the door. The arch was cut on a band saw and hand-routed, with laminated back banding....It was more time-consuming than I originally imagined."

Above left: Dala horse *Below:* Swedish wooden kitchen implements.

ESBJORN

CARL

ULF

SUZANNE

BRITA

Des Moines artist Stephen Hay did all of the Larsson reproduction painting, duplicating different images from Larsson's paintings and from Sundborn itself, incorporating them onto the cabinets and the built-ins in the Swedish Room.

"Fellow artists Rebecca Ekstrand and Tom Rosborough painted with me…and selflessly offered hours of advice and the impartial perspective of fresh eyes. And with Mrs. Ahmanson's enthusiastic guidance and support, the preliminary designs grew into a reality which hopefully brings something of the charm of Carl and Karin Larsson's lifework to the hotel and its guests."

The *pièce de résistance* is surely the bathroom door, which is painted with a striking reproduction of a portrait Carl Larsson did of Karin. Like every other detail in the Swedish Room, it transports you to another time and place.

Left: Detail of hand painted cabinets by Stephen Hay. Images reproduced from Carl and Karin Larsson's home. *Above right:* Detail of door panel featuring reproduced portrait of Karin Larsson.

Stephen Hay
Des Moines, Iowa

Stephen Hay was trained at the American Academy of Art in Chicago, and in private study at the Atelier Lack in Minneapolis, where Richard Lack, a representational painter, was his mentor. He also studied independently at the British Museum and the Victoria and Albert Museum in London and in Athens, Greece. He received a grant from the Iowa Arts Council to work with restoration painters in the Governor's private office in the State Capitol and studied at the Isabel O'Neil Foundation in New York, which is dedicated to the art of painted finishes. There he learned gilding and decorative work with traditional materials. He now owns and operates Stephen Downing Hay Fine Art and Decoration.

"Carl Larsson and his wife Karin were the premier Swedish Arts and Crafts artists, and all of the painted images in the Swedish Room of the Hotel Pattee were derived or adapted from the Larssons' work in Sundborn, their country home. Carl's habit of painting portraits of his family on door panels is translated here onto the built-in units as well as the copy of Karin's portrait on the vestibule side of the bathroom door. The pattern on the vestibule walls comes from a Larsson watercolor of his children's bedroom.

"The design and sayings over the arched vestibule doorway we reinvented from old watercolors Larsson painted of his dining room, while those on the opposite wall above the cabinet are taken directly from existing work. The frieze is a mélange of flowers from a border in their daughter Suzanne's bedroom, various flower studies of Carl's, plus 'Gods Peace' from the dining room, and a compressed version of the 'welcome' painted over the exterior front door to their house. Even the window alcove bears a quatrefoil portrait Larsson did of his four older children, balanced by an oak leaf garland, which frames an interior window in their home. For the proverb above the built-ins and window alcove, quoted in Swedish, the letterforms are adapted from the roundel he painted on the ceiling of the guest room."

Stephen Hay also contributed to the Mexican, the William Morris, and the King's Daughters Rooms in the Hotel Pattee.

William Morris Room

The Arts and Crafts Movement, which Carl and Karin Larsson interpreted in Sweden, began in England in the Nineteenth Century with the writings of a British philosopher and critic named John Ruskin who argued that human design should reflect Nature in its form. It should use natural, handmade materials and should respect the creativity of the craftsmen and women who implement its design. Mid-century, Ruskin's students formed a group of artists, writers, and designers who sought to find expression for his ideals. One of them was named William Morris, and his name came to be synonymous with the Arts and Crafts Movement that he launched.

During the restoration of the Hotel Pattee, one of the architects searched the collection of the Iowa State Historical Society in Des Moines and found an article that provided a very detailed description of how the Pattee brothers had designed and furnished the hotel.

It reported that they had visited the LaSalle Hotel in Chicago and were impressed with the English Arts and Crafts architecture in one of its public rooms, and they decided to make the interior of their hotel in that style.

Roberta Ahmanson was intrigued by the article. But, she points out, "It's *English* Arts and Crafts, which is an important thing to remember. Not American. And if you are going to do English Arts and Crafts, you ultimately go to William Morris. So I decided we had to have a William Morris Room."

A year after the hotel opened, in March of 1998, Mrs. Ahmanson met Elaine Hirschl Ellis, who had been recommended through the Museum of American Folk Art in New York City. After a visit to the Hotel Pattee, Ellis thought the Morris room needed a more authentic treatment.

In their effort to improve the authenticity of the room, Ahmanson and Ellis went to England. In describing their first trip there, Elaine Ellis says, "I took her to a couple of people who were doing craft work — Chris Vickers in particular, but some others as well. I said 'You've got to see the pieces. See how they are made. See the context in which they were planned.' After we left Chris's, I was thinking it would be really nice if Chris could make pieces for the Morris Room because he does beautiful work. And she said, 'Do you think you could get him to do some work for the room?' So it was like a meeting of the minds."

Christopher Vickers is a contemporary fine woodworker in the Arts and Crafts manner. He does all his work in a little shed behind his house in Somerset, England.

Roberta Ahmanson: "Chris made the beds, which he designed after the stair rail in Morris's Red House. There are English-style chairs that are known as Morris chairs. He made a painted cabinet, which is a replica of the cabinet that's at the Victoria and Albert Museum, and an Englishwoman did the painting on it. Christopher also designed a desk, another knockoff of the stair rail in the Red House, to fit with the rest of the furniture."

The backgammon cabinet, a reproduction of an Edward Burne-Jones design, was painted by Sonia Demetriou, who describes the uniqueness of the project: "I have spent the best part of the last thirty-odd years painting and decorating furniture and restoring painted furniture. …I have painted many pieces that have been copies of original designs in one form or another. I have decorated many harpsichord cases, one of which was commissioned by the Sultan of Oman, decorated in gold leaf with scenes of the Oman landscape and buildings. But I have never been asked to copy such an elaborately decorated piece as the backgammon cupboard.

"…I set about researching both the artist and his work by looking at illustrations of his paintings, I learned that there was a pencil drawing of the backgammon players, done as a study for the cupboard, in the storerooms at The Fitzwilliam Museum in Cambridge,

Above left: Burne-Jones's backgammon cabinet reproduced by Christopher Vickers, painted by Sonia Demetriou.

so I arranged to visit this to make a close study of the details and requested a large commission photograph as reference. In the storerooms of the Victoria and Albert Museum in London, there are several pieces of furniture painted by Burne-Jones, which I also made a special request to visit, to give me a rough idea of style and technique.

"I received the cupboard direct from Christopher Vickers in non-primed wood state, smelling beautifully of cedar. I prepared it for decoration by painting with several coats of oil-based paint and, where necessary, filling any wood grain. The background to the sides and legs is gilded with 22-carat gold leaf. The decoration is painted with oil paints on top. It was a very enjoyable project, the final article giving the impression of a very rich tapestry."

Once the construction of the new furniture was under way for the William Morris Room, a different wallpaper was sought, fashioned after that in Morris's own bedroom at Kelmscott Manor in England. And draperies were designed, based on a Morris wall hanging.

"Morris was one of the people who brought back embroidery," Roberta Ahmanson explains. "For the Red House he designed a crewel embroidery hanging of daisies. He and his wife Jane embroidered it, and those hangings are in Kelmscott Manor. Elaine Ellis went to the Royal School of Needlework at Hampton Court Palace and asked them to make a kit of those hangings, which they did. Elizabeth Elvin, the school's principal, went to Perry in the spring of 2000 and trained local women to do the embroidery. So six women

from Perry and the surrounding communities did the embroidery on the hangings, which are now the drapes in the room."

The light fixtures in the room are original W.A.S. Benson lamps, designed of copper. "When we looked into whether to buy reproductions or to use the real ones, we found it was cheaper to buy the real ones. So we may have America's largest collection of Benson lamps in that room." Benson designed lighting for Morris and Co. for many years.

Carpet was replaced; two authentic Sussex chairs — based on a medieval design — were added. William Morris was also a calligrapher, and artist Stephen Hay copied a Morris piece depicting the seasons. Every detail of the William Morris Room has been laboriously researched and painstakingly reproduced.

Morris is often quoted, "Have nothing in your homes which you do not know to be useful or believe to be beautiful." The room at the Hotel Pattee that bears his name is not only authentic, but it is useful to design connoisseurs and world-weary travelers alike. Above all else, as he would have hoped, the William Morris Room is beautiful.

Left: Original W.A.S. Benson copper lamp.

Elaine Hirschl Ellis
New York, New York

Elaine Hirschl Ellis has been an active enthusiast of the Arts and Crafts Movement for more than two decades. In 1980 she curated "Gustav Stickley: A Celebration of Quality" and co-produced the accompanying film. In 1987 she established the Craftsman Farms Foundation and organized the successful effort to acquire and preserve Craftsman Farms, the home of the designer Gustav Stickley. Purchased by the Township of Parsippany, New Jersey, the museum, which opened in April 1990, is administered by the Foundation of which Ms. Ellis was the founding chair. More recently, it is to the British designers and architects that her interests have turned. She started Arts & Crafts Tours in 1992 as a way to share her combined love of England and the Arts and Crafts with others.

Gustav Stickley Room

VOL. VIII, NO. 2   MAY 1905   35 CENTS

THE CRAFTSMAN
GUSTAV STICKLEY, PUBLISHER

The Marquis Ito By Dr. W. E. Griffis

CONTENTS

If William Morris is the central historic figure in English Arts and Crafts, the same can be said for Gustav Stickley — who was born to German parents in Osceola, Wisconsin, in 1858 — in terms of American Arts and Crafts. Because of his contributions to America's movement and because of the German immigrant community's contributions to Perry, Iowa, the Gustav Stickley Room pays tribute to both.

Many ethnic groups came to farm the rich soil in Iowa. But no one could farm quite like the Germans. In some instances, they found themselves trying to raise crops on land that had been overcultivated, abused, and abandoned by others. With skills learned through centuries of agrarian European life, they knew how to rejuvenate exhausted soil and undo the damage others had done. Their crops thrived. And just as important to state and local economies, they knew how to operate profitable farming businesses.

But Perry's connections with the German community run even more deeply than that. In the Stickley Room are photographs of a woman named Maria (Seifert) Bills, who, as a child, was on her way to a German death camp. She and her sister were almost miraculously rescued from the train and in the months and years that followed began a new life in Perry. Maria grew up, married, and eventually received the Business and Professional Women's Mother of the Year Award in 1992. Maria Bills, like so many other German immigrants, personified the American dream.

It has been said that Stickley, born to German immigrant parents, created the first truly American furniture, known throughout the world as "Craftsman" style. A trip to England in 1897 inspired Stickley, after seeing William Morris's work, to create a new line of handcrafted furniture based on Arts and Crafts principles. Fueled by the belief that art should reflect people's everyday lives, he adapted the English style and began to produce an indigenous American interpretation. His magazine, *The Craftsman*, first published in 1901, provided patterns for building houses. To this day they stand as examples of Craftsman architecture, which has its Midwest interpretation in Frank Lloyd Wright's Prairie Style. The Stickley room is furnished with reproductions of Gustav Stickley designs.

Wisconsin artist Amy Miller stenciled a handpainted border around the frieze. "We chose an original Arts and Crafts stencil design called Rose and Bellflower," Miller explains, "which truly complemented the room. Authentic period stenciling techniques were achieved by using oil-based paints in earth-tone colors of burnt umber, yellow ochre, olive green, and barn red.

Above left: Cover of Stickley's magazine, *The Craftsman. Below:* Photograph by Edward Curtis.

The stencil paints were applied with flat-tipped stencil brushes, and the oil-based medium allowed the freedom to blend the colors softly, back and forth, creating beautiful, subtle effects within the stencil pattern."

Gustav Stickley often used American Indian artifacts and textiles in his decor, and this adds another design element to the room. There is a Navajo rug on the floor. On the walls are six historic Edward Curtis photographs. Curtis spent thirty years photographing North American Indians. In the process, he produced more than 3,000 images, including some eighty different tribal groups.

Elaine Ellis, who helped develop the William Morris Room, also worked with Roberta Ahmanson on the Stickley Room. Of the textiles in the room, she says, "They were done by Ann Chaves who is from Pasadena and is probably one of the most creative, imaginative, and skilled of the American embroiderers. Her work is exquisite. She did the window hangings and the pillows for the bed, with the idea of using themes that would have been Arts and Crafts, specifically about nature."

Left: Detail of Ann Chaves needlework.

Ann Chaves
Pasadena, California

Ann Chaves's Arts and Crafts resource, Inglenook Textiles, specializes in custom, one-of-a-kind art needlework. Of her work at the Hotel Pattee Ann Chaves writes,

"Normally I do not do reproduction work. However, when I was invited to create textiles for the Gustav Stickley room, I readily agreed that some of the designs needed to be from Gus's Craftsman Studios. The portiere pod design was chosen because of the wonderful movement of the stems, which fit so well with my own love of movement in design. I checked The Craftsman *magazine and found that Stickley was not severe about the colors to be used and suggested using colors that were appropriate to the setting. I then chose a linen fabric that has a rather handwoven look, which Stickley loved.*

"I was also asked to create three pillow designs and make two pillows with each design. When I asked what plant forms would be appropriate, the obvious answer for a hotel in Iowa was, of course, corn. Since I normally draw and photograph the plants that I design from, I knew that this request would be a challenge. There's lots of corn in Iowa…but I live in Los Angeles! Cornfields are very rare.

"Then, to my surprise, a close friend who lives in my neighborhood decided to plant her entire urban front yard in corn! I spent several days traipsing through her yard photographing, drawing young plants, and thinking about Iowa. While stitching I remembered the wonderful visits to the Hotel Pattee and the women I met who love needlework. The kits I made for the Hotel Pattee gift shop were made with them in mind."

RAGBRAI/BRR Room

No matter where people come from, the more they become acquainted with Iowa, the more they love it. And there is no better way to get to know Iowa — and Iowans — than by riding in the RAGBRAI® bicycle tour. Pam Jenkins describes the event.

"There you are, riding with 10,000 people on bikes in the hot summer. And everyone speaks to you. Everyone is helpful. There is food everywhere. It's a party, but it's a uniquely Iowa party. There are about 10,000 people on bicycles, far more people than live in many of the small towns that they ride through. The townspeople whose towns you ride through are excited to see you. They welcome you. They want to hear your story. We would ask the farmers, 'How many hills are left?' and they'd say, 'Only one more.' Well, there were twenty more. But RAGBRAI® was all about that kind of hospitality and warmth."

The "Register's Annual Great Bike Ride Across Iowa" was started in 1973 by *Des Moines Register* feature writer/copy editor John Karras, an avid bicyclist, and Donald Kaul, writer of *The Des Moines Register*'s "Over The Coffee" column. The ride attracted between 300 and 500 bicyclists the first year and is now limited to 8,500 participants for reasons of safety. The tradition is to put your bike's back wheel in the Mississippi and its front wheel in the Missouri. This means that you've completed RAGBRAI®.

BRR (Bike Ride to Rippey) is another story. Roberta Ahmanson describes it, "BRR is done in the first weekend in February every year – rain, shine, snow, sleet, hail, whatever. And people get a little inebriated. Some of them never leave the pub. They're getting anti-freeze, and some of them just stay for the anti-freeze and forget the ride. But about 1,500 people actually ride in this crazy thing. And they're nuts. But it's fun."

Visiting the RAGBRAI/BRR Room at the Hotel Pattee may be almost as much fun as setting out on one of the rides. Primary colors, black-and-white photos of life on the rides, embroidered patches, bedspreads marked like the highway, and lots of folk and fine art capture the spirit of biking in fresh country air, summer or winter. California artist/sculptor Rob Brennan, known for sculptures made of found objects, created the headboards, tables, and several of the lamps using various bicycle parts and pieces, including a unicycle and a water bottle. Perry folk artist Betsy Peterson put one of her Humpties on a bike in the niche, and Mary Kline-Misol painted the frieze mural, showing the route of both rides along with portraits of people who made them happen.

She has a special place in her heart for RAGBRAI® because her father worked at *The Des Moines Register* and was involved in the race when it first began.

Tracie McCloskey says, "The pillows are all made out of old T-shirts and sweatshirt logos that were taken from the ride. The desk chair was done by Boris Bailey, who made it out of old bike path signs. There's a unicycle, a bike pump, and bike gears, which Rob Brennan used to make lighting fixtures. We had so much fun designing the RAGBRAI® Room!"

Above left: Betsy Peterson, *Biker with Dog,* 1997, mixed media, 16 inches high. *Above right:* Detail from Mary Kline-Misol frieze featuring BRR. *Below:* Patch from RAGBRAI-V, 1977.

Southeast Asian Room

Roberta Ahmanson admires needlework. And the needlework displayed in the Southeast Asian Room is striking for its intricate detail and perfect execution. Vibrant designs in fabric, thread, and yarn bring to the prairie the stories of Laos and its neighboring Southeast Asian countries.

At the end of the Vietnam War in 1975, Iowa was one of many states that took in refugees, and some of them came to Perry. A Vietnamese woman, Thuyen Tran, has worked for the Hotel Pattee since 1998. Later on, in the early 1990s, Iowa Beef Packers (which is now owned by Tyson Foods) brought Laotians into the area to work at the pork plant, and some of them still live in Perry.

"Perry has Southeast Asian immigrants in its history," Roberta Ahmanson points out, "and there are people in town today who came from there, so we needed a room to remember them and to honor them. The Southeast Asian Room has an old Southeast Asian wedding chest and Filipino baskets. There are two Indonesian shadow-puppets, which were a gift from our friend Paul Marshall. They were made by Edhy Wahyudi who makes the puppets for the performances in the royal palace. The room also has a wonderful collection of Hmong needlework done by an Iowa woman named Susan Her."

Her's needlework represents her Hmong tribe's exceptional skill and precision in embroidery. She is a master in the art of Hmong *paj ntaub*, which means flower cloth, and is pronounced "pan dow." She is passing this tradition on to young Hmong immigrant women so her culture's traditions will not be forgotten. Her work was featured at in the Des Moines Art Center's Iowa Artists 2000 exhibit.

Hmong "story cloths," like those displayed in the Southeast Asian Room, are intricately stitched, telling stories of war, migration, and resettlement.

The art was learned in Laotian homes and later in refugee camps as the displaced tribespeople awaited transport. Now that they are resettled, however, young women are not learning the art of *paj ntaub*. This is a loss, because the needlework is a chronicle of the Hmong people's hardship and struggle. But in the Southeast Asian Room wall hangings and needlework squares have survived to document these pieces of the world's history, "written" in thread and fabric by women at the end of their long journey to America.

Above left: Southeast Asian wedding chest. *Below:* Detail from story cloth embroidered by Susan Her.

As Barry Kemp and R.M. Harvey demonstrate — and we'll see more examples as we continue to tour the Hotel Pattee — the visions of small-town men and women sometimes carried them far away, exposing them to opportunities and experiences they could hardly have imagined possible. But some of those dreamers stayed in town, and besides fulfilling their own dreams, they also brought gifts of imagination and creativity to all who knew them.

Such a woman was Betty Mae Harris, whose dance studio in Perry, Iowa, taught many a generation to move with grace, to feel the beat of the music, and to enjoy the sound of applause for a good performance. Roberta Green Ahmanson remembers her well.

"Betty Mae Harris was famous in Perry. She taught dance for thirty-seven years, and a good proportion of those thirty-seven years she taught dance in what had once been a café on the second floor of the Hotel Pattee. When we started renovations of the hotel, it was still decorated to be Betty Mae Harris's dance studio with ballet bars on the wall and big frosted globe lamps from the '60s, which were the size of basketballs and in vivid colors. Betty Mae taught dance there until 1961. I thought that she needed to be remembered as a piece of Perry's culture."

Betty Mae Harris was born in Harlan, Iowa – the daughter of a Baptist minister. After performing with the Ziegfeld Follies, she relocated to Perry and established her dance studio. A glance at the dance programs displayed on the walls of the room reveals that her classes were very sophisticated for their time. As Pam Jenkins points out, "Look at the costumes and the kind of detail. She's kind of a precursor to these beauty contests that travel around the country now. You look at her makeup and her hairstyle. This woman was reading *Vogue*. She was up on the times."

The Betty Mae Harris Studio is decorated in a feminine style — abounding in floral fabrics and ruffled trims — and contains scrapbooks of the beloved dance teacher's decades in Perry. The costumes displayed on the walls are changed, with the seasons, four times a year. And innumerable photographs and programs recapture the spirit of her work in Perry.

Pam Jenkins: "She had an idea that elegance and beauty could be portrayed in dance, and she found a niche here and thrived here. And young girls were so proud to be part of her, they speak of her with this incredible love. What she taught them was how to walk, how to talk, how to be in front of an audience. It's an amazing kind of story that so many parents, in this town of mostly working-class people, were proud to send their kids to be taught by her."

Above left: Betty Mae Harris, c. 1941.
Below: Program from Betty Mae Harris Spring Dance Recital, 1948, and Hawaiian hula skirt c. 1941.

Chinese Room

As the Hometown Perry, Iowa researchers worked to piece together fragments of the region's past, they discovered that a Chinese man named William Arshong had owned and operated a market in Perry in 1875. They also found evidence of a Chinese hand laundry and of another family with a Chinese surname. This and the fact that today there is a Chinese restaurant in Perry raises the question of Chinese immigration to Iowa in general, and Perry in particular.

No one is quite sure how or why Chinese immigrants arrived in Dallas County, Iowa. "But we do know that there was this man who had a store," says Roberta Ahmanson. "He was a little odd from what I've been able to read. So I thought that we ought to remember the Chinese heritage, too."

As the decor for the Chinese Room was envisioned, Roberta donated from her private collection embroidery pieces that she had first purchased in Hong Kong. She added a seriograph of Jan Kasprzycki's watercolor "Star Ferry, Hong Kong." The room contains traditional Chinese folk dolls and a

contemporary Chinese teapot. But its most dramatic artifact is a 1920s Chinese robe from Beijing.

The robe once belonged to Virginia Olson Green, Roberta's mother. During the 1920s, Virginia's great-aunt, Louise, was married to an attaché for the U.S. Commerce Department to the U.S. Embassy in Beijing. When she returned to the United States, she brought a few treasures home, such as the robe.

The Chinese Room has a decorative frieze, bordering the ceiling with red, yellow, and green Chinese bottles framed in black. And, thanks to Tracie McCloskey, a hand painted parasol has been redesigned into a ceiling lamp, providing one final touch of light and whimsy.

Above left: Contemporary Chinese teapot. *Above:* Vintage Chinese robe. *Below:* Room detail with print (Jan Kasprzycki, *Star Ferry, Hong Kong*).

Alton School Room

even included high school students.

Pam Jenkins describes country schoolteachers: "Because of the nature of having to teach so many age groups at once, there were never quite enough teachers. I interviewed a woman who taught in 1922 in a country school. She described her day: She got up in the morning, fed her horse, attached it to the buggy. She rode to the school, tied up the horse, and once she had started a fire inside the schoolhouse, she was ready to teach. And she got no help from her husband, because she wasn't allowed to have a husband. Once you got married, you couldn't teach. Teachers had to be single women or men. For example, the woman I'm talking about taught school for three years from 1922 to 1925. Then she married and her teaching career was over."

In today's Alton School Room are photos of the old, functioning school along with pictures of Abraham Lincoln and George Washington. A map of Iowa from the Carnegie Library is displayed on the wall, along with a forty-eight-star flag — throughout nearly all the years Alton School was in operation, the United States had only forty-eight states. A slate chalkboard and abacus are framed, hung above a desk similar to those in the Alton School. Nearby is an antique pendulum clock.

The artifacts in the Alton School Room were present as innumerable children passed through the schoolhouse doors. Nor were all those students native Iowans. The challenge of teaching students of every age was sometimes complicated by the arrival of immigrants.

Y ou're probably beginning to see that the themes of work, family life, faith, and loss repeat themselves again and again in the rooms of the Hotel Pattee. And education — the fifth theme, so important to Iowans — is the focus of the Alton School Room, named for the one-room school that operated in Perry from 1867 until 1961. You will recall that we first glimpsed it in Bobbie McKibbin's painting in the Dallas County Boardroom.

Iowa has long been a leader in American education. When settlers arrived, they formed communities based on faith, ethnicity, and other commonalities. Once these communities grew large enough, a country school was founded, usually in one classroom, instructing students from first through eighth grades. Sometimes the classes

For example, a group of Bohemians settled near Perry some time in the late Nineteenth Century, including some young men in their twenties. When work in the mines ceased, the young men decided to learn English at the local one-room school. The teacher was stretched to the limit by this added responsibility, but she somehow did it all. For her, the school was a center of learning for the entire community, and it was up to her to provide all the basic educational tools necessary to prepare young men and women for the future — a future that might well carry them far beyond the prairies.

Above left: Contemporary photo of Alton School House. *Below:* Antique abacus.

Russian Room

Although the Russian community in Iowa is not large, for nearly half a century the state has had a unique relationship with that country. While traveling in Europe early in 1959, Roswell and Elizabeth Garst, who owned a huge farm near Perry, visited with the premier of the then-Soviet Union, Nikita Khrushchev, and his wife. As the couples said their goodbyes, Elizabeth Garst invited the Khrushchevs to visit them in Coon Rapids, Iowa, should they ever come to the United States. All of them must have known that this was a rather unlikely scenario during those Cold War years.

To the amazement of many and the consternation of not a few, Khrushchev and his wife did indeed visit Iowa in late summer, 1959. The man who represented the "Evil Empire," as Ronald Reagan later described it, was driven through Iowa's small towns in a motorcade. He was surrounded by eager paparazzi, creating one of the first true media events of its kind. Roberta Green remembers it well.

"I was one of the schoolkids who stood on Willis Avenue and watched as Nikita Khrushchev went by. I couldn't really see him because he was on the other side of the car. My father had said that he 'wouldn't walk across the street to see that man.' He went to the dump that day. When he was coming back, he stopped at the stop sign. He couldn't get back on to Willis Avenue to come home and instead found himself within five feet of Khrushchev. So my mother always said, 'Yes, you wouldn't walk across the street, but you would drive all the way across town to see Nikita Khrushchev.'"

In fact, Iowa has much in common with Russia and Eastern Europe. The land is similar, and the tradition of agriculture is the same. Despite the debate surrounding Nikita Khrushchev's visit to Iowa, it was a small step toward greater understanding. And today, the conversation among farmers around the globe has expanded and is perhaps more important than ever. In Pam Jenkins's words, "Khrushchev wanted to come to a farm because he understood the value of farming. Perry and Coon Rapids are small towns, but throughout the history of the small town, there have always been global connections. His visit was just another one."

After the end of the Soviet Union, Russia once again became a sovereign state. The Russian Room is decorated in the manner of Old Russia, fashioned after the dacha, the Russian summerhouse, dating from the early 1800s. The frieze is painted with the Cyrillic Russian alphabet. A dramatic hand painted Romanoff bed was custom-built for the room. Authentic Slavic shawls are draped as window coverings. Russian Orthodox icons are on display, and some of the pillows are made from old vestments.

Russian artist Oksana Sokolovskaya's "Babushka Knitting" dominates the north wall. The pleasant-looking, silver-haired grandmother looks almost alive as she focuses on her handwork. She, too, provides a link between Russian and Iowan cultures because the tradition of rural women working with their hands goes back as far as history can carry us.

Above left: Icon of St. Nicholas, the patron saint of Russia. *Below:* Photograph of Nikita Krushchev's visit to Iowa, 1959.

American Indian Room

The fabric of American Midwestern life is interwoven with a diverse array of men and women from a variety of immigrant cultures. But with all the ethnic groups in Perry — be they Russian, Swedish, German, Southeast Asian, or Irish — the story of Perry, Iowa, would be incomplete without including the American Indians. Stories of the American frontier and Lewis and Clark's expeditions in search of a Northwest Passage cannot be retold without paying tribute to the Indian tribes that populated the prairies before the Europeans moved westward.

Often these people are referred to as Native Americans, but in Roberta Ahmanson's words, "When we were doing research about this, Pam Jenkins and I went to the Autry Museum of Western Heritage and everything was labeled 'American Indian.' This seemed wrong, so we asked the curator. He said, 'They mainly call themselves Indians.' Later I saw that an Apache who worked for us, named Ruben Grijalva, had a bumper sticker that said 'Indian and proud of it.' It was always clear to me who he thought he was. It didn't say 'Native American and proud of it.'"

The Indians who live in Iowa today are primarily of the Sauk and Mesquaki tribes. There is a community in Tama County, Iowa, which was settled by a group of Indians representing four tribes— Kickapoo, Pottawatomie, Sauk, and Mesquaki. Under the leadership of several progressive leaders including Chief Pushetonica, a group of displaced Indians actually used their U.S. government annuities to buy back their own land in the Nineteenth Century — an unusual and progressive step for a people who had been disenfranchised by American expansion. But all the tribes that once lived in Iowa have not returned. For example, although there are "Ioway" tribes in Nebraska, Kansas, and Oklahoma, the U.S. Government does not list Ioway Indians in the state of Iowa.

The American Indian Room at the Hotel Pattee recalls the cultures of tribes not only from the Plains States, but also from across the United States. There are Lakota Sioux artifacts in the room — these Sioux once lived in and around Iowa, hence the cities named Sioux City, Iowa, and Sioux Falls, South Dakota. The room's drapery rods are fashioned of arrows and arrowheads. In the room are three Sioux Indian costume dolls, including a papoose, created by Randy Charging Bear Williams, who is known for making dolls in authentic costumes, with beading and feathers.

Navajo blankets hang on the walls. Seriographs by Jack Silverman depict Indian textiles. And carved of painted leather by Des Moines artist Will Ghormley, is a portrait of Sitting Bull, Lakota Medicine Man and Chief, who was the last Sioux to surrender to the United States Government.

Above left: Will Ghormley, *Sitting Bull*, 1997, leather, 16.5 x 12.5 inches. *Below:* Indian doll by Randy Charging Bear Williams.

Irish Room

May the Sun shine warm upon your face, th

"May the road rise to meet you. May the wind be always at your back. May the sun shine warm upon your face, the rain fall soft upon your fields, and until we meet again, may God hold you in the palm of His hand." So reads the Irish blessing that is painted around the frieze in the Irish Room.

The Irish are a people of many blessings, and they formed a large community in Iowa — a community that grew dramatically in the mid-1800s. During those years, several counties in Iowa reported as much as 17 percent of their population being born in Ireland. An 1846 article describing people best suited to emigrate from Ireland to Iowa said, in part,

"…Those who have been accustomed to a country life, and to the labor of a farm, are, of course, better fitted to cultivate land and endure hardships…. Married persons are generally more comfortable, and succeed better, in a frontier country, than single men…. Many is the wife, whose cheerful countenance now gladdens the fireside of the 'Iowa farmer,' that once beamed brightly in the gray saloons of the crowded city."

The Irish farmers, accompanied by their wives of "cheerful countenance," made their way to Iowa, and there they stayed. They brought with them their Roman Catholic faith, built churches and schools, and found their place in the community. Irish immigrants worked to establish their roots and remember their traditions.

In Perry, the Irish and German immigrants helped to build the Catholic Church of St. Patrick, where the first mass was celebrated in 1871. The original wooden church was a haven to arriving immigrants who found comfort in their faith. The present St. Patrick Church, which was opened and dedicated in 1902, continues to welcome new immigrants from Central and South America.

Irish immigrants also helped to build schools. The O'Malleys, for example, were one of the founding families in the Perry area. Nora O'Malley worked throughout her life to build a Catholic school for her children and for other families. St. Patrick School was dedicated on February 21, 1921, and remains a vital part of the community.

It is no surprise that Roberta Green — whose surname reflects her father's Irish (albeit Protestant) roots — heard enough Irish tales from her paternal relatives to know that, given their contribution, there would have to be an Irish Room in the Hotel Pattee. She and Tracie McCloskey worked together to create an atmosphere similar to that of an Irish cottage. The walls are whitewashed with a heavy plaster, and the fabrics are plaids and tweeds from Ireland. An antique Irish headboard graces the bed, and Irish lace hangs in the windows.

Finishing touches include a pair of dolls from Dublin; a Claddagh mirror from Ahmanson friends Maura O'Neill and Michael Harnett, who stayed in the room at the hotel's grand reopening; Waterford crystal and Belleek china; a calligraphied rendering of the "Breastplate of St. Patrick"; and a quote on the wall from William Butler Yeats, one of the Twentieth Century's greatest Irish poets. It says, "Tread softly for you tread on my dreams," a phrase with which people — whatever their national or ethnic or religious background may be — can surely identify.

Above left: Kitty Whelan, *Kilkeasy*, 1994, appliqué, embroidery, and quilting, 34 x 38 inches. *Below:* Detail of Irish Room. *Next page:* Detail from *Garden Party at Ram House* by Rosemary MacCarthy-Morrogh.

Irish Needleworkers

Rosemary MacCarthy-Morrogh

Rosemary MacCarthy-Morrogh's first works in textiles began when "I made strange things for my small daughters, puttering along on my own." Soon after, the Irish Patchwork Society was formed and she realized that there could be more to her needlework than she had imagined. Now she thrives on generating ideas and constructing them. She has explored creating very large textile pieces, but also enjoys making small things, especially bags and jewelry. Her work has been exhibited in Ireland, Germany, Austria, and the United States.

After a time of study at the Tyrone Guthrie Artists' Retreat at Annaghmakerrig, MacCarthy-Morrogh has been developing cutwork techniques, creating art that is rich in texture and intricately worked. Her methods have changed over the past ten years, from batik and patchwork into increasingly personal, innovative forms, combining hand and machine stitching, dyeing, and beading. Representing this genre is "Garden Party at Ram House," which hangs in the Irish Room at the Hotel Pattee. Here MacCarthy-Morrogh combined machine appliqué on linen, hand and machine embroidery, cutwork, cording, and beading.

Monica Tierney

Monica Tierney grew up in a small picturesque town called Bunclody, in County Wexford, located on the southeastern corner of Ireland, its long coastline bordering both the Irish and Celtic Seas. Her textile art has evolved from her work as a painter, and she joined the Irish Patchwork Society with the aim of translating her existing work into a different medium.

Tierney says that she has a flair for visual expression that needs to be spontaneously and imaginatively expressed. "The free expression of this gift is as necessary to me as sleep," she says. She finds that discussion and exchange with artist friends is also extremely helpful, and she encourages them to give her the critical feedback that she needs to continue to grow as an artist.

"Much of my work has focused on the landscape of Ireland. Some of the pieces that portray the green fields of Ireland I refer to as patchwork fields." Displayed in the Irish Room at the Hotel Pattee is "A Wexford Farmstead." Rendered in hand painted cotton, hand appliqué, and embroidery, it is a work that clearly reflects this vision. Tierney hopes that in some way she is preserving a picture of Ireland's countryside before industrial development causes irreversible damage to its beauty. She and her husband live in Blackrock, a seaside suburb of Dublin.

Kitty Whelan

"I must have been born with a needle and thread in my hand because I do not remember a time when I didn't knit and sew," Kitty Whelan says. Over the years she has studied and practiced a variety of textile media including embroidery, tatting, and lace-making, as well as other visual arts such as oil painting and flower arranging. "Along the way my eye was developing color and design skills, while my hands were accomplishing a variety of techniques."

In the 1980s, when a revival of patchwork was sweeping Great Britain and Ireland, Whelan became an early member of the Irish Patchwork Society. In 1990, she spent time at the Tyrone Guthrie Artists' Retreat at Annaghmakerrig, in County Monaghan. Here she explored her Celtic heritage and found it inspirational for such textile designs as those on disply at the Hotel Pattee.

"Jerpoint" is an impressionistic view of the ruin of Jerpoint Abbey which still stands in County Kilkenny. "Kilkeasy" is named in memory of Whelan's father's birthplace. In this piece, the rural setting is symbolized by a mythical bird motif, and the area's ancient history of monastic settlement is remembered in the Celtic knotwork around the border.

Mexican Room

Until the late Twentieth Century, the only Latin immigrants in Perry were spouses of local people who came north to be with their partners. There was little history of Mexican or Central American family migration. But all that changed in 1989 when Iowa Beef Packing bought a meatpacking plant that had once been owned by Oscar Mayer. IBP has since been purchased by Tyson Foods.

When IBP advertised in Mexico and California for workers, a flood of immigration began to wash across the region, and it dramatically changed the demographics of the Perry area. Many local people assume that these immigrants are all from Mexico, and some are. But, in fact, they represent nine different Spanish-speaking countries. Today one-third of the children in Perry schools are Latin.

Roberta Ahmanson says, "Around 30 percent of the Hotel Pattee's employees are Latin American, and many of them are Mexican. So they are an important part of life in Perry, and there needed to be a room in the Hotel to honor them."

After deciding on a Mexican Colonial style for its decor, the Mexican Room was coated with heavy plaster, washed in a golden hue, and artist Stephen Hay was commissioned to create a border design that would incorporate floral images, typically found in Mexican folk art. (See more about Stephen Hay on page 51.)

The beds were hand carved, too, and hand painted by a group of Mexican artists. Their firm, Art Antiqua, is internationally recognized, having designed some of Pope John Paul II's private rooms. The carved headboards reflect botanical shapes that are woven into the red damask bedspreads, and several antique pieces, including the desk chair and a lamp, add to the rich ambiance.

A rosary, an embroidered wall hanging of the Virgin of Guadalupe, and a ceramic Noah's Ark are among the room's collection of artifacts. Most notable is a painting, "Taxco Church" by Millard Sheets, who was perhaps California's best-known Twentieth Century watercolorist.

"Millard Sheets," Roberta Ahmanson says, "who was a great friend of my husband's late father, was a founder of the California watercolor school. He used to take people on painting trips to paint different places in the world. On a trip to Mexico, he painted the cathedral."

Above left: Ceramic Noah's Ark.
Below: Millard Sheets, *Taxco Church*, 1970, watercolor on paper, 22 x 30 inches.

Central American Room

J ust steps away from the elegance of colonial Mexico is a room so imaginative and vibrant that at first you might not notice the geckos. And it's true that geckos aren't the kind of creature some people enjoy having in their bedroom. Even the fact that they eat mosquitoes may not have convinced you that they make good roommates. If so, you haven't seen the Central American Room at the Hotel Pattee. The room's brightly painted geckos are not only companionable, but they complete an already lively room with a touch of wit — not to mention the fact that some people believe geckos bring good luck.

It was certainly good luck that so many diligent workers from Central America came to the Hotel Pattee to help make guests comfortable. Like their Mexican cousins, they arrived in the surrounding areas during the 1990s to work in the IBP facility, arriving from places like Guatamala, Honduras, El Salvador, Panama, and Costa Rica. And when the Central American immigrants came to America, like the Hmong tribeswomen from Laos, they brought with them their needlework skills.

The fabric molas and woven pieces in the Central American Room at the Hotel Pattee are intricate and colorful.

They provide contrast with the brightly painted walls, and a backdrop for purple, orange, and red accessories. A wooden parrot, a Guatemalan flag, and a mosaic mirror create an ambiance at once joyful and beautiful. Inside a Plexiglas™ box is a Costa Rican gourd, which opens to reveal tiny depictions of the Biblical creation story on one side, and the Nativity on the other, a treasure brought home by Howard Ahmanson.

Perry artist Betsy Peterson was invited to add folk art touches to the Central American Room's decor. Roberta Ahmanson describes the results, "There are geckos on the mirror in the bathroom, and geckos, of course, you find in tropical places. So when you sleep in the Central American room, the geckos are with you. The room itself is folk art. It's quite wonderful."

Above left: Costa Rican gourd featuring Nativity and Creation scenes. *Below:* Detail of gecko by Betsy Peterson. *Next page:* Third floor stairway landing with painting (Gary Bowling, *Prairie Fields and Horizon*) and "Humpty" (Betsy Peterson, *The Engineer*).

Betsy Peterson
Perry, Iowa

Betsy Peterson, who has lived in Perry, Iowa, since she was five years old, has always been surrounded with originality and invention. "I grew up in a very creative home," she explains. "Mom brought us five children up to enjoy thinking creatively and trying to solve problems creatively. Later, I went to art school and really enjoyed drawing and hand building clay things."

Today the Peterson farmhouse is filled with the colorful folk art and the interesting pottery that have made Betsy and her husband Eric Peterson well known in Perry, Iowa. Betsy's most recognizable pieces are the sculptures she calls "Humpty Dumpties," fashioned of found wood, fabric, and imagination. Eric is a potter, and the Petersons' family environment is one in which their two sons are able to "learn to think outside the box and experience the freedom to try new things—good new things."

Betsy Peterson has been involved not only in the creation of Humpties, but also in the expressive atmospheric touches that have added personality and charm to the Snick Hamlin Room — a vivid blue Dinny the Dinosaur, and the Central American Room — several friendly gekkos.

George and Agnes Soumas Suite

WITH GOD NOTHING IS EMPTY OF

Many small American towns proudly claim their own war heroes — brave soldiers, marines, airmen, or sailors who fought valiantly in one of the nation's military conflicts or wars and thus received national recognition. But very few communities have a local hero whose story has been recounted in Hollywood cinema, his real-life role reenacted by George Segal. The film "The Bridge at Remagen" recounts a battle fought late in World War II, one of whose most decorated warriors was a man named George Soumas. George was the son of a shoe-repair man, and he lived most of his years in Perry, Iowa.

The Soumas family's background was Greek, and George Soumas, who returned to Perry to become a lawyer after the war, had a manner that was molded by his ethnicity. Pam Jenkins says, "His way of doing business in the world was through building relationships. Other attorneys remember that there would be a line of lawyers at the Dallas County Courthouse in Adel, waiting to see the judge. George would just walk right up to the front.

"He was also the police judge in Perry, and when young kids got in trouble for the first time, sometimes he would overlook the violation. He would let them go the first time if he believed in the kid. People would come and say, 'You know, Mr. Soumas, I messed up,' and he would yell at them and then tell them what to do."

People still fondly recall George Soumas sitting at a table with his coffee cup with a group of men at a morning coffee meeting, and a statue of him — coffee cup and all — is installed in the Soumas Court, on the east side of the hotel. George Soumas played many roles in his long Perry history. Twice he was mayor of Perry, and in later years he was responsible for seeing that Highway 141 to Perry was widened to four lanes.

Because of Soumas's importance to the town of Perry, Roberta Ahmanson says, "I thought it was appropriate to name a suite after the Soumases. And because he was Greek American, the rooms were made to look like a Greek island house. One window has a jalousie-like window treatment. The rooms are decorated in fabrics that are traditional to island Greece, and the bedroom has the kind of iron bed you would find in a Greek home."

When you enter the Soumas Suite, you step onto a mosaic floor, designed of river stone. Before you, in a Plexiglas™ box, is George Soumas's World War II U.S. Army uniform, a reminder of his heroism. As you walk inside the living room area, you encounter an eclectic array of Greek furnishings and accoutrements in the manner of a Mykonos country house. Two paintings by Jan Kasprzycki capture contemporary Grecian scenes, and frescoes recall several wise sayings of the ancient world — from both Greek philosophers and early Christian thinkers.

Photographs of George Soumas abound, documenting his life as a soldier and his years served in the practice of law. Alabaster ceiling lights and seashell lamps illuminate the suite, and icons of St. Stephen and St. George are hung on either side of the bed, offering silent blessings in the Greek Orthodox tradition. Those two saints, beloved heroes of the Eastern-rite Christian community, embody the courage, character, and valor that motivated George Soumas himself — no matter what the cost.

Above left: George Soumas's World War II army uniform. *Below:* Soumas Suite living room with antique jalousie screen.

Travel Suite

Like the Kids' Suite on the Second Floor, the Travel Suite was designed and installed by Sticks®, and a riot of color, form, and imagination is the happy result. The king-sized headboard serves as a centerpiece and sets the mood for the rest of the suite, celebrating life's journeys. In a sweep of color behind the bed is the sun, setting in a sapphire sky, while a crescent moon rises along with myriad stars and clouds, envisaging a sleepy traveler's dreamscape.

The hand painted furniture, the colorful airplane quilts and pillows, and the John A. Bayalis, Jr. painting, titled "Geography Lesson," all conjure up faraway places with strange-sounding names. It is difficult to imagine a more appropriate theme than travel for a hotel suite, but it isn't just those who visit the Hotel Pattee who experience *wanderlust* and find their way on the highways and byways of the world.

"People from the Midwest travel," Roberta Ahmanson points out. "I think they may even travel more than anybody else because they are landlocked and they want to see what's out there. And my father was one of those people. He started traveling when he was

fifteen years old, and so I grew up traveling. Every summer we looked forward to our vacation. We traveled all over America."

The Travel Suite sleeps four — besides the king-sized bed there is a trundle bed in the second bedroom, so it is ideal for families on the go. And the contemporary folk art style is an ideal complement to both the Travel Suite's theme as well as to the Arts and Crafts motif in the Hotel Pattee.

As Sticks' designer Sarah Grant-Hutchison says, "Mrs. Ahmanson was not afraid to integrate into the hotel's architecture artwork and installation works that have nothing to do with that

architecture. I mean, if the whole hotel were strictly "period," Sticks would not be there. She was very clear from the beginning that this was going to be a marriage of those two things. Which I think makes it more interesting than if it had gone one way or the other — completely nouveau or completely period. She didn't do either one."

It's true. Whether you are an art aficionado, a travel expert, a design critic, or simply a weary pilgrim glad for a night's rest in cheerful room, the Travel Suite offers the best of all worlds.

Above left: Detail from Sticks® cabinet panel.
Above right: Headboard and canopy by Sticks®.

Telital Room

Nearly every city, town, and village in America has a local newspaper, and nearly every high school has its own student publication. Perry, Iowa, is no exception. The *Perry Chief* has been the town's paper since 1874, keeping its readership up to date on weddings, births, and deaths, the wins and losses at local sporting events — all the essential events and insights that matter most to the Perry community. And the *Perry Chief* has long published on its back page the *Telital* — or "Tell It All" — the student paper (known as the *Chief's* papoose) that has documented the life of Perry High School's students since 1926.

Having spent many years as an award-winning newspaper reporter, Roberta Green Ahmanson has a special love for journalism. She says, "When I grew up, the *Perry Chief* was the *Perry Daily Chief* and was published every day but Sunday. Now it is published weekly. As a kid in high school, I worked at the *Perry Chief* after school. I was the person people called to find out why their paper wasn't there. I'll never forget it. It was very important to me."

She also studied journalism in high school and was therefore involved in the production of the Perry High School *Telital*. "I chose 'Telital' as the theme for the room because I worked on the paper and because the first few friends I ever had were other people who were involved in journalism. Leonard Rossman was Perry's journalism teacher from 1929 to 1967 and he was a formidable personality. He really gave me the career that I later enjoyed so much as a reporter."

One of those "first few friends" young Roberta Green found in journalism class was Pam Jenkins. Of their teacher Leonard Rossman, Pam says, "He was a real stickler for correct grammar, correct spelling, getting the story right, for checking your sources. Students not only had to write articles, they had to go down to the *Chief* and copyedit and proofread these articles.

He really took the old school approach to journalism, and he saw himself as training professional journalists."

The Telital Room evokes the mood of 1930s films such as "Front Page" or "Girl Friday" with Cary Grant and Rosalind Russell, with the role of the hard-bitten journalist who wore a trench coat and pounded out late-edition stories on a manual typewriter — the cutting-edge technology of the day. The room's frieze is composed of early images from the *Telital* and displays a collection of artifacts including antique cameras, an early radio, and an old telephone. Above the bed are three photographs illustrating First Amendment cases with ties to Iowa that went to the U.S. Supreme Court and appeared in the *Des Moines Register*. One of these photographs, of Amish children climbing a fence, won a Pulitzer Prize.

A life-size trench coat, carved of wood by Laguna Beach, California, artist Rene Megroz, hangs near the door. And enshrined in an end table is an old manual typewriter, bearing silent witness to the never-ending stream of news stories that, for nearly eight decades, has filled the pages of the *Telital*.

Above left: Vintage typewriter.
Left: Leonard Rossman, c. 1960.

V.T. "Snick" Hamlin Room

Do you remember Alley Oop? Whether because of the comic strip or the humorous 1960s popular song that parodied it, most people do. On August 7, 1933, a caveman named Alley Oop first appeared in America's newspaper comics. Not long thereafter, Alley encountered a dinosaur named Dinny, and the two formed a partnership — Alley Oop not only rode on Dinny's back but adopted him as a pet. The two prehistoric characters were always getting into trouble in the Land of Moo's jungles, where danger lurked and not-so-friendly dinosaurs threatened. Later Alley and a lovely cave girl named Ooola fell in love, and other characters began to come and go. Eventually a time machine entered the picture, and Alley Oop and friends were surveying the modern world from their prehistoric vantage point. All this colorful activity was brought to the world by Vincent Trout Hamlin, who was born in Perry, Iowa, in 1900. Family members called young Vincent "Snick," and although he never really liked the nickname, it stuck.

Hamlin, like many young men of his generation, fought in Europe during World War I. After the armistice, he returned to Perry. He then went on to Drake University, where he studied journalism and worked as a reporter for the *Des Moines Register*. Eventually Hamlin moved to Texas.

There Alley Oop appeared.

The familiar theme of imagination carrying a small-town boy or girl into a different world is nowhere more evident in the Hotel Pattee than in the Snick Hamlin Room. Roberta Ahmanson describes the idea behind the decor: "Snick Hamlin lived some of his years in Perry in an Arts and Crafts style house on Willis Avenue. In the room, all the things that are related to his life in Perry are in natural wood or natural wood frames, reflecting the Arts and Crafts style of his family home. But those things that came out of his imagination are in vivid color."

Not only are the colors vivid, but thanks to Perry folk artist Betsy Peterson, an enormous blue Dinny the Dinosaur dominates the room. The two queen-sized bedspreads were copied from a bedspread that actually appeared in an Alley Oop comic book. The room's borders are a collage of Alley Oop comic strips, and framed episodes of Alley Oop's adventures hang on the walls. Photographs of Hamlin, pages of the Perry High School Yearbook, and U.S. Postal Service stamps record the biography of the Midwest region's world-famous cartoonist.

About the impact Hamlin's background made on his work, Pam Jenkins says, "Early in this century, where you were from was important in defining yourself and your art. You see it in philosophy, you see it in art such as Grant Wood's, you see it the writings of Hamlin Garland and Willa Cather. You see this idea that if you lived in a place, that place would produce a certain kind of thinking. In the high school yearbooks V.T. Hamlin worked on, those *Blue and Whites*, as they were called then, you see his talent. And so even though he never came back to live in Perry and even though his main character was a prehistoric character, his work still reflects the values and beliefs of a small town."

With that in mind, and because creativity and imagination always enliven the ordinary world, a drawing pad and colored pencils are available to guests who stay in the Snick Hamlin Room. At no extra charge, and just for fun, they can express their own bright ideas. And more often than not, they do.

Above left: V. T. "Snick" Hamlin, c. 1935.
Below: Room detail including Alley Oop print and original Alley Oop comic books.

Marching Band Room

Along with colorful leaves and the smell of wood smoke in the air, one of the much-loved harbingers of autumn in America is the sound of the high school football game — the roaring crowd, the chanting of cheerleaders, and the music of the marching band. From parades to pep rallies to concert performances, marching bands embody school spirit and community pride. And perhaps because of Meredith Willson's musical comedy "The Music Man," Iowa seems to epitomize the magical allure of snare drums, glockenspiels, "Seventy-six Trombones," and all the other instruments that march along beside them.

Recalling her years growing up in Perry, Roberta Green Ahmanson says, "Every little town in Iowa had a marching band. Every high school had a marching band. Sometimes the police had their own marching band. The firemen had a marching band. Even churches had them. People had marching bands, and marching bands are a piece of Midwestern culture. Perry, Iowa, restored its band shell and they started having band concerts not long ago, and now people come out in large numbers. And why not? It's wonderful! It's fun music and people love to hear it.

People think, we may be in Iowa, but through the magic of music we are connected to a larger world."

Because Iowans love marching bands, of course the Hotel Pattee needed a Marching Band Room. And the room is, in Tracie McCloskey's words, "over the top." The room's showpiece, designed by California artist Rob Brennan, is a headboard constructed entirely of band instruments. Brennan recalls, "Tracie told me the theme and I thought, A marching band? How am I going to do a marching band? I was at such a loss to figure something out. Then I thought of the glockenspiel — it has such a nice, stylish shape. But just finding one of those things is really hard. And they're not cheap either. All the instruments I used are working instruments. But once I found the glockenspiel, then the rest really kind of came together."

The headboard is an amazing piece of creative ingenuity, but it's only the beginning. The room's lamps are fashioned out of other band instruments. The desk chair is upholstered to look like the uniform of a marching band musician, and the room's drapes are similar, with martial-looking gold pullbacks. Artist David Kreitzer's delightful painting, called "Uncle Milt" and his frieze mural of marching bands complete the room's celebration of Midwestern music.

"The Marching Band Room is one of my favorite rooms," Pam Jenkins explains, "because the room is just whimsical. And one of the things you see in that room is this belief that music and art and cultural things are important in small Midwestern towns. There's always been this belief that kids should learn an instrument. And there's always been this idea that pig farmers and railroaders and merchants and laborers could appreciate and understand music."

Above left: Detail of headboard by Rob Brennan.
Below: Perry Municipal Band, c.1900.

Bill Bell Room

It is a long journey from the local Iowa marching band to the New York Philharmonic Orchestra. It is an even longer journey if your musical instrument of choice is a tuba. Most people associate the "oompah" sound of the tuba with, at the very best, a John Philip Sousa concert in the park on the Fourth of July. But one man successfully made that journey from the Midwest to New York. Not surprisingly, he was an Iowa tuba player who had a close association with Perry.

Bill Bell was born in Creston, Iowa, which is a town a little larger than Perry in south-central Iowa. For eighteen years he played tuba for the New York Philharmonic. In fact, many people agree that he was the man who made the tuba a symphony instrument. And Bill Bell died in Perry, Iowa. He moved there to live with his sister during his final illness and stayed until the end of his life.

Bell's biographer, Harvey G. Phillips, writes, "When William Bell was around ten years old, he began playing tuba in a boys' band in Fairfeld, Iowa. The leader of this band was a local grocer with some musical training. It must be pointed out that in the early part of the century, every town of consequence had its own town band made up of adults and accomplished younger musicians. These town bands had enthusiastic and loyal fans in their respective geographic areas….The State of Iowa has always been renowned for its bands and output of great brass, wind, and percussion players. Young Bill Bell's person benefited greatly from the enormous pride expressed by Iowa's citizens for their native bandsmen."

Acknowledging Bell's fame, Roberta Ahmanson says, "Because of his musical accomplishments, we named a room after him. He's buried in Perry and famous tuba players sometimes come and play their tubas around his grave. We have Tuba Day every year. And because Bill Bell was a gentleman, we thought the room should be done very 'Gentlemen's Quarterly.'"

Indeed, the Bill Bell room is both masculine and sophisticated. It is decorated with Biedermeier furniture, including a leather headboard that is black and brown and a leather chair. The art in the room is limited to photos of Bill Bell — but they are wonderful photographs, thanks to the generosity of the New York Philharmonic. They, of course, wanted to honor Bill Bell, too. Also displayed on the walls are some of Bill Bell's album covers.

And then there's the tuba.

"It's a King tuba," Tracie McCloskey explains, "and there are very few of them in the world. Fortunately, we were able to find one and we had it mounted by Rob Brennan to use as a piece of sculpture in the corner."

Bill Bell's story is another version of the vision that moved people from the Midwest into the greater world.

And he serves, too, as an example of the value that Midwestern people place on cultural activities. Even though work, faith, and family have always been at the core of their lives, small-town Americans have always recognized the value of art and music and theater. "The stereotype of the rural Midwest was that people were not very sophisticated," Pam Jenkins points out. "But there were clubs that read Shakespeare at the turn of the century. There were people who listened to classical music. There have always been Midwesterners who appreciated all varieties and levels of culture."

Bill Bell, the elder statesman of tuba music, was certainly one of them.

Above left: Bill Bell album cover.
Below: Carnegie Hall program, 1948-1949.

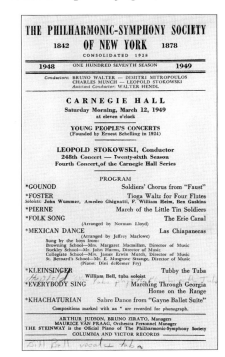

Louis Armstrong Suite

From the marching band to the symphony, musicians are highly regarded in Iowa's cultural scene. So is it any wonder no one has forgotten Louis Armstrong's fabled visit to Perry, Iowa? And after playing his trumpet at Lake Robbins Ballroom — a venerable performance venue six miles from Perry — where else would Louis Armstrong have lodged during his 1950s Iowa performance but at the Hotel Pattee?

Those were the days, of course, when rampant racial segregation still marred America, and many hotels did not welcome black artists. As Pam Jenkins explains, "While the black community in Iowa might not have faced overt hostility and violence, it certainly experienced prejudice and discrimination. But when Louis Armstrong came to stay, I don't think there was ever a question about whether he could stay in the Hotel Pattee and be part of the community. People went to see him and they saved their tickets because it was such an important event. They still remember when he came."

The Louis Armstrong Suite is a memorial to the great jazz trumpeter and his origins, so it is decorated in a New Orleans style with a heavy French accent. The drapes are velvet, and the ornate touches include a wrought iron bed, faux marble trim, and red crystal lamps. Above the fireplace is a Louis Armstrong poster, and several more are hung throughout the suite, along with photographs, concert tickets, and a hand-kerchief, which serves as a reminder of Josephine Lee's note to the jazz great (see page 139).

Left: Louis Armstrong announces one of his numbers, on stage at a Baltimore theater during a personal appearance in 1950.
Below: Detail of Armstrong Suite living room with fireplace.

African Room

Louis Armstrong's experience in Perry, Iowa, where he found himself welcome at the Hotel Pattee, was not only the result of his celebrity. Iowa was far more gracious to blacks than some of its neighboring states. Around 400 African Americans settled in the Perry area toward the end of the Nineteenth Century, either to work on the mines in Angus or on the railroad. Pam Jenkins describes their circumstances:

"There has always been an African American presence in Perry from almost as far back as the 1870s. I think the first blacks came in the 1890s as the railroad came in. There were two black churches very early on, as early as the 1900s — the African Methodist Episcopal (AME) church and a Baptist church. And there are stories of both community support and discrimination. When the Klan was popular in the early 1920s, Cy Oscars tells a story about his mom, who was a cook for the Hotel Pattee. The Klan burned a cross in her yard. She went out with a shotgun and told them never to come back. And they didn't.

"Gail Davis, a black man who came back from World War II, tells a different story — he says that he could have lived anywhere, but came back to Perry because, he said, 'I could go into a grocery store without a dime and get a loaf of bread on my name.'"

In recent years, Africans have arrived — Sudanese and Somalians — who made their homes nearby. Although the Sudanese population was larger early on in the 1990s than it is now, some of them continue to work at the local pork plant.

The Hotel Pattee's African Room was created to honor those African immigrants as well as the African-Americans in the community. Describing the indigenous fabrics in the room, Tracie McCloskey says, "While we were designing the room, I met this woman from Mozambique who was importing, not just from Mozambique but from different parts of Africa. We got all of our fabrics through her. But we did the upholstery, chairs, bedding, and pillows ourselves. There's a grain door that's really beautiful, an African shield over one of the beds, and the Ndebele doll that Roberta found."

It is a dramatic room, dominated by a magnificent sculpture of a Zimbabwean bushman by artist Adam Mdabe. Mdabe recycled the remains of vehicles that had been abandoned after the civil war in Zimbabwe more than a decade ago and made sculptures of human beings out of them. One of his works is this life-size bushman, who kneels on a bench next to one of the two beds.

Of this unique piece of artwork, Roberta Green Ahmanson says, "Maybe it was the most audacious thing that I did in the whole hotel." Perhaps so, but along with the mosquito-netting bed canopies and the shields from various African tribes, the room has the feel of an authentic African locale. Guests could very well think of it as a sort of mini-safari — a virtual visit to an exotic travel destination without the bother of passports, visas, vaccinations, or airline tickets.

Above left: African drum. *Below:* Ndebele doll.

King's Daughters Room

Cultural change, social concern, and care for the unfortunate don't just happen. And it is no secret that women have a special gift of seeing needs and finding a way to get things done about them. Sometimes women of faith decide to address the needs of their community — blending their faith with energy and practical efforts. When they do, dramatic results often follow. So it was with the Protestant women's auxiliary King's Daughters in Perry, Iowa. The King's Daughters not only reached out to the hurting, but they also built a hospital in which to care for them. Roberta Green, among many other Perry natives, was born in that hospital.

But Roberta Green's birth was not the event that put the King's Daughters Hospital in the history books. The best-known thing that ever happened there involved the infamous gangsters Bonnie and Clyde and their reprobate relatives and friends. Bonnie and Clyde, along with Clyde's brother Marvin (known as Buck) and his wife Blanche, were known as the Barrow Gang. On July 29, 1933, having stolen a car in Perry and recovering from wounds sustained during a previous shootout, the Barrow gang was camped out near Dexter, Iowa, in an abandoned amusement park. A posse opened fire on them. Bonnie and Clyde escaped, with Clyde carrying Bonnie slung over his shoulder. Blanche was captured. Buck Barrow was wounded. He was rushed to the hospital — the King's Daughters Hospital in Perry, Iowa. And he died there.

In the Hotel Pattee's King's Daughters Room, framed newspaper articles recount the saga of the Barrow Gang's demise. It is a rough, violent end to a sordid tale. Thankfully, the King's Daughters room itself tells a far different, far gentler story. The room itself is a feminine extravaganza — lavender and pink and white. Crystal lamps gleam; ladies' hats, purses, and gloves and other accessories grace the walls. The decor abounds in ruffles, lace doilies, and overstuffed chairs.

Designer Tracie McCloskey says, "My favorite things in the room are David Krietzer's watercolor paintings. One is titled 'Ladies Aid,' and the other 'Women and Children First: The Lunch Line, Christ Church, Cairo, Nebraska, 1946.'" The paintings are hung over the four-poster beds.

On one wall of the room is a Maltese cross, an important King's Daughters symbol, bearing the letters I.H.N., which stand for "In His Name." Some of the organization's oft-quoted credos are painted in script above the wainscoting, such as "Not To Be Ministered Unto But To Minister." Perhaps most telling is the King's Daughters motto: "Look Up, Not Down; Look Forward, Not Back; Look Out, Not In; Lend A Hand."

Despite its brief flirtation with a rowdy passage of gangster history, the King's Daughters story is a noble one, and the King's Daughters Room at the Hotel Pattee is a peaceful place. It abounds in the kinds of furnishings and accoutrements that the women who built the hospital would have appreciated and thoroughly enjoyed.

Above left: Ladies' vintage handbag and gloves.
Below: David Kreitzer, *Women and Children First: The Lunch Line, Christ Church, Cairo, Nebraska, 1946,* 1997, watercolor on paper, 27 x 39 inches, *detail.*

Quilt Room

Life, like the fields, would be dull without peaks and valleys.

Few things are more reminiscent of country living than quilts. For centuries women all around the world have made quilts to keep their own families warm and sometimes to provide extra money for the food budget. In more recent years, art quilters have created fabric designs that are far too exquisite to be used as bedding. Whatever the purpose of the finished product, quilting has long been a way for women to express themselves when other forms of expression were unavailable. And it often provided women with a productive and enjoyable social occasion—quilting bees gave them an opportunity to talk to other women, to exchange the news of the day by getting together, and to make good use of their time. Because of that, and because quilts are beautiful, Roberta Ahmanson decided that the Hotel Pattee should have a quilt room.

"Quilts were always a part of life," she explains, "because quilting was a way to make something beautiful out of odds and ends that you had left from other things that you had made. The patterns, of course, became famous for the stories they tell, just as the people who make them sometimes became famous as quilters."

When deciding about the kind of decor that would best provide a setting for the quilts to be displayed, Tracie McCloskey took a 1930s farmhouse approach. "We did that so we could just keep layering. And the concept of the miniature quilts was to display as many quilts as we could by as many artists as possible."

Twelve quilt squares — the "miniature quilts" Tracie mentions — represent the personality and style of a dozen gifted quilting artists. Most are fabric; two are made of paper — one of Iowa postage stamps, the other of origami farm animals. Prominently displayed on one wall of the room is a large quilt that won first prize at the Iowa State Fair in 1999. An ambitious project by JoAnn Belling, the quilt took nine years to complete. It is a dramatic work with a black background and jewel tones of sapphire, amethyst, ruby, and emerald. Jacobean textile design describes a specific style of floral appliqué, and JoAnn Belling's quilt features flowers and birds, thus inspiring its name, "My Jacobean Garden."

When designing the Quilt Room, Tracie McCloskey says, "First of all, we wanted to show quilts. The desk and chair were custom made and painted to depict a crazy quilt. A furniture designer, Robert Harman, made the big reclining chair with the look of a contemporary quilt."

An antique crazy quilt is suspended from the ceiling, and a quilt hangs as a backdrop behind each bed. Virginia Green, Roberta's mother, made the quilt squares that decorate the dust ruffles for the two Jenny Lind beds.

Award-winning quilter Murray Johnston, whose work is displayed in several rooms of the Hotel Pattee, sums up the spirit of the Quilt Room from her perspective,

"One of the aspects that I have always found fascinating about quilts is that they reflect the life and the environment of the maker. Be it the rocky road to California, the monkey wrench used to build the barn, the schoolhouse their children attended, the flowers and the gardens surrounding the home, or the sunshine and shadow on the cabin wall, the quilts were an attempt to put beauty into the most utilitarian of objects. Even though often unsigned, quilts are a testament to the creativity and artistry of their anonymous makers, stitched often in the most straitened of circumstances with recycled supplies. The pride in the workmanship is obvious and the search for new patterns, color combinations, and ideas is never-ending. I feel that I am only continuing the centuries-old tradition of expressing myself in cloth and like to feel that my quilts pay tribute to the women who came before."

Above left: Kathyl Jogerst, *Amish Square in Square,* 2000, quilt, 16 x 16 inches. *Below:* Quilt rack.

Needlework Room

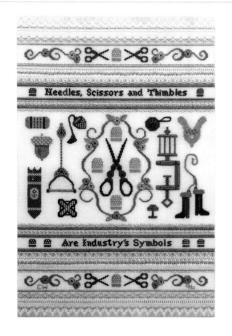

As Murray Johnston has said, throughout the centuries needlework — including, but not limited to quilting — has been created, usually by women, to add beauty to their homes and to express their creative impulses. We've already seen in the Southeast Asian and Central American Rooms that even in cultures where there is little leisure time or extra money, women continue to create strikingly beautiful works with their hands. Patterns, colors, and techniques are passed down from one generation to the next, and the finished products not only represent nationalities and ethnic groups, but serve as a common language among the peoples of the world.

Although we know that needlework is an ancient craft, because of the fragility of fabrics and threads, few examples of early work remain, although some have survived in Europe, such as the Bayeux Tapestry in France (also called the *Tapisserie de la Reine Mathilde*), dating from the Eleventh Century. With the emergence of the Arts and Crafts Movement in the Nineteenth Century, embroidery experienced a renaissance as a response to the industrial revolution and the bad machine work that it produced. William Morris and his colleagues researched medieval needlework designs and began to reproduce them. Because of their influence and the Arts and Crafts theme at the Hotel Pattee, it was only right that a guest room should be devoted to needlework.

In the room that bears its name in the Hotel Pattee, needlework is everywhere. One wall is devoted to Iowan artisans and includes weaving, tatting, and embroidery. There is a sample of bobbin lace, which is very difficult to produce — in fact, it is almost a lost art. Over the beds are samplers. There is also an example of metal-thread work, which is another subset of embroidery. "The only piece in the room that I know was made by a man," Roberta Ahmanson says, "is a pipebag purse made by a Chippewa Indian man."

Another wall features international needlework and includes pieces from all over the world, including a Transylvanian vest, needlework pieces from South America, and samples of Brugges lace from Belgium, the recognized home of great laces. Laces from Galicia in Spain and embroidered pieces from Greece hang alongside contemporary needlework from England.

The room is designed to focus full attention on a wealth of fine handwork that surrounds the beds, desk, and chairs. Above the wainscoting is a hand painted border by Mary Kline-Misol, rendered in oil paint, of a traditional topiary lace pattern. Dark wood furnishings contrast elegant off-white bedding accented by crochet, myriad samples of intricate needlework, and a collection of colorful handmade pillows.

Roberta Green Ahmanson says, "The Needlework Room is one of my favorites because embroidery thrives in the Midwest as well as other places all over the world. I embroider myself. I'm not very fancy, but I do it for therapy. And, in fact, one of my cross-stitches is in the room."

A good friend of the Hotel Pattee is Elizabeth Elvin, the principal of the Royal School of Needlework located at Hampton Court Palace in England. She has conducted needlework classes at the hotel and oversaw the Daisy Hanging reproduction project in the William Morris Room. She is an impassioned champion of needleworkers. "Embroidery is an art form rather than a craft," she explains. "A lot of women do it as a pastime, and they think it doesn't matter, and that they aren't really artistic. But they are. The art is in the design and color and texture. Needleworkers bring all that to life."

Above left: Collette Wortman, *Stitcher's Sampler*, 1998, embroidery on canvas, 15.5 x 22 inches.

Chautauqua Room

hat men should do
Matthew 7:12

If at first you don't succeed, try, try again.
– McGuffey's Fourth Eclectic Reader

"The Chautauqua is the most American thing in America," President Theodore Roosevelt once exulted. Today his statement may sound like a rather peculiar expression of national pride. But he was talking about an education and entertainment phenomenon that took the United States by storm in the late Nineteenth Century, only to lose its momentum with the advent of motion pictures.

In 1872, John H. Vincent of Camden, New Jersey, was a young Methodist minister and the editor of *The Sunday School Journal*. In an effort to bring Sunday School teachers together for all-day training, he organized a gathering in the lakeside New York town of Chautauqua. Within two years, the daylong session had expanded. Women, men, and children began to gather for several days beside Lake Chautauqua for summertime entertainment, food, and lodging. From near and far they arrived, and the subject matter quickly moved beyond religious teacher training to include music, plays, and lectures on a variety of subjects. By the turn of the century, similar gatherings were taking place all across the country, often meeting in large circus-style tents. In the movement's glory days, there were 21 different Chautauqua companies, and their events were attended by 35 million people.

A man named C. Durant Jones was a leader in the Temperance Movement.

He also owned one of the largest Chautauqua franchises in the nation and built the Jones Building in Perry to house the Chautauqua offices. At one time, the enterprise was the second largest employer in Perry — second only to the railroad. Numerous people from Perry traveled and performed in Chautauqua programs.

Of the movement's impact on Perry, Iowa, Pam Jenkins observes, "The Chautauqua brought to Perry nationally known speakers, it brought theater, it brought musicians, it brought poetry readings, and it brought people who looked forward each year to Chautauqua coming. It also, of course, had a spiritual connotation. It was a way for people to be reflective about their lives and who they were. And what's interesting to me about this is that there's a strong tradition in the Midwest of learning and education, and Chautauqua is an example of that."

Since the Chautauqua played an important part in Perry's cultural history, the Hotel Pattee has a Chautauqua Room. Tracie McCloskey explains its decor, "Because the Chautauquas took place in tents, we wanted to give that feeling to the room, so we used awning fabric behind the bed to create a canopy and did the roll-up shade like a stage coach shade or a tent shade. For the furniture, we used a rustic style because the Chautauquas began in outdoor camps."

The room contains a David Kreitzer painting reminiscent of the times, depicting a gathering of men and women in their 1890s summer attire, chatting beneath shade trees with white Chautauqua tents in the background. Another painting, by Steven Kozar, depicts the Jones Building in Perry. And, lest anyone forget the Chautauqua's humble outdoor beginnings, two throw pillows on the bed are decorated with ants — those ubiquitous picnic party-crashers.

Above left: Chautauqua program, 1915.
Below: Chautauqua program.

Woodworking Room

When women arrived in Iowa, they brought with them their time-honored abilities in quilting, needlework, and other fabric-related skills. When men arrived, they often brought other gifts, including their talent for woodworking. All of these aptitudes celebrate a way of life immigrants had long honored in the "old country." Today, those crafts are still popular, reflecting the creativity and personal expression that is connected to both work and leisure.

Woodworking sometimes resulted from the reality that men and women earned their living with their hands. But more often, Perry, Iowa's farmers, railroaders, and pork plant laborers demonstrated in their woodworking an artistic impulse that they simply could not express in their daily labor. And just as with other handcrafts, some of the products of the woodworkers turned out to be art.

The Woodworking Room in the Hotel Pattee honors contemporary woodworkers from the state of Iowa. Chris Martin who teaches at Iowa State University in Ames, Iowa, near Perry, designed the room concept and several of the unique furniture pieces in the room. Of the project, Martin writes, "In addition to the creation of the Woodworking Room, I feel the best thing to come out of this project was the development of bonds between craftspeople from around the state. As I worked with the other furniture makers, I gained profound respect for them. I was also pleasantly surprised to find the deep pool of talented craftsmen and artists that exists here in Iowa."

A group of other very talented woodworkers participating in the room added their unique style to the design and construction of each piece. These include a table and nightstand by Eric Hansen of Iowa City, who describes his work: "The design scale and material made hand tools the heart of the project.... Jack planes, chisels, and Japanese saws allow for an intimacy between medium and creator that makes an unmistakable signature....Craftsmanship, time, and interest combine to form skill. That skill and a little luck results in functional sculpture only hand and heart can create."

Above left: Hand carved wooden duck.
Below: Detail of bed with cherry, mulberry, and chickory woods designed by Chris Martin and crafted by Chadwick and Bergstrom Furniture.

Two lamps were made by Thomas Monahan of Cedar Rapids; cabinets by Chadwick and Bergstrom Furniture of Des Moines; and the desk and chair were made by Jeffrey Hayes.

A rocking chair and footstool were created by Gene Hancer of Sioux City. The back and seat of the rocker are maple burl. Ebony was used for the toenails, along with Carpathian Elm and Fiddleback maple for the remainder of the chair and stool.

Paul Iverson of Lake City writes about his part of the project — an easy chair and ottoman. "The chair and ottoman are made of white oak, and the pieces were form bent. The front and rear legs were shaped by hand. These were the most challenging parts. I have been building furniture for seventeen years as an independent craftsman. I credit God with my talent, and my work experience in a millwork shop … for the development of my skills."

The room's frieze is a painted pictorial of the woodworking process by Carl Homstad of Decorah, Iowa. On a wall are large portraits by Linda Shackelford, a freelance Iowa photojournalist who photographed the woodworkers using their tools to create the furniture and artifacts in the Woodworking Room. Jeff Easley of Wellman, Iowa, created the wooden frame around the portraits.

Roberta Green Ahmanson describes what is, for her, the most significant display in the Woodworking Room. It hangs above a workbench by Eric Pereza. "On one wall is a container that looks like an opened-up carpenter's case. It's almost like a triptych you would see in a church or a chapel, except it contains tools. The tools that are in this case were my father's tools. And I think it's a fitting honor to him to hang his tools on the wall in the Woodworking Room. My dad loved to work with wood and built things everywhere he went. That was his craft. The Woodworking Room honors him and all men like him who built houses and cupboards and shelves, who could fix things, but who also built beautiful, carved artifacts. That's what the Woodworking Room is about."

Left: Detail of display case by Eric Pereza with Earl Green's tools. *Below:* Lamp by Thomas Monahan.

Eric Pereza
Moffat, Colorado

"*I worked with Mrs. Green to gather up her husband's tools, and put them into a permanent display case. I got inspiration from Mr. Green himself. I imagined, if he'd had his own workbench where he could work with his tools, what it would have been like. And that's the way I built it. I think he would have liked it. It is a privilege to have known him.*" Eric Pereza also constructed the futon pedestal, the table, and the Tansu cabinet in the Japanese Room and has worked on projects in many other rooms of the Hotel Pattee.

"*I was born in Honolulu, Hawaii, where my father and his three brothers are union carpenters. Three days after high school graduation in 1969, I entered a carpenter's apprenticeship program, and after four more years I began to work as a journeyman carpenter. My experiences in woodworking are many and varied, extending from high-rises in Waikiki, to custom homes on the California coast, even to custom doghouses that can withstand the Colorado winter. It has been a special privilege for me to apply my trade to several of the rooms in Iowa's extraordinary Hotel Pattee.*"

Amana Colonies Room

Old World woodworking is just one of many other skills — clockmaking, crafts, weaving, the preparation of meats and cheeses, bread baking, winemaking — that the founders of the Amana Colonies in Eastern Iowa brought to the Midwest from Germany.

In 1714, Eberhard Ludwig Gruber and Johann Friedrich Rock founded a religious group, the "Community of True Inspiration," in southwestern Germany. After experiencing religious persecution, the small sect left Europe to find a safe haven in the United States. Around 800 Germans established the first of the Iowan Amana villages in 1855. Before long, seven villages were formed on 26,000 acres in the Iowa River Valley of Eastern Iowa.

The villages were surrounded by huge fields and are said to have been an hour's oxcart drive apart. The villagers were very strict, pietistic Christian believers who isolated themselves from the larger Iowa community. Their communal way of life finally came to an end during the Great Depression in 1932 they began to interact with their Iowa neighbors. Restaurants, museums, and hotels opened; historical tours were organized, and shops made handcrafts

available. Today the Amanas welcome more than 1.5 million visitors each year.

In 1934, George C. Foerstner founded Amana Refrigeration, which was to become the most widely known business that emerged from the Amana Colonies. In 1967 they introduced the now-famous Amana Radarange Microwave Oven.

It is, however, handcrafts and other old-world skills that best reflect the traditional Amana Colonies' culture. Tracie McCloskey describes the process of decorating the Hotel Pattee guest room that honors the Amana Colonies. "We went to the antique dealers and picked up the Bible and the songbook and the old cape; also some blocks that were made for printing cotton calico fabric, which are displayed in the room. The carpet was actually woven by a husband and wife in the Amana Colonies.

On the walls are photographs of old Amana along with collages of letters, crocheted work, and other memorabilia from Sandy Tschopp's "My Amana Series."

Of the Amana Colonies Room at the Hotel Pattee, Roberta Ahmanson says, "Someone connected with the Colonies' Heritage Association came and stayed and checked out the room for us to make sure it was appropriate. Now they come every year during Oktoberfest, and we have more Amana food than we normally have on the menu. We have German music and beer, of course. Sometimes there's a yodeler and accordion player. We have this German experience in Perry, Iowa, thanks to the Amana Colonies who are our friends."

Above left: Antique prayer shawl from the Amana Colonies.

Sandy Tschopp
Marion, Iowa

Sandy Tschopp was born and educated in Iowa. As part of her graduate program in education at the University of Iowa, she studied the creative process and the understanding of metaphor. Her interests in metaphor and photography converged when she began making still-life images and photomontages. In "My Amana Series," the artist examined letters and pieces of handwork done by women in her family at the turn of the Twentieth Century. The images in this group of photographs are all sepia-toned and printed on textured paper. Of the collection, Ms. Tschopp writes,

"My Amana Series was conceived to recognize the creative energy of women, especially that of past generations, when marriage and motherhood were the only paths open to most. Objects chosen for the still-life images refer to the traditional outlets women have used to satisfy their need to create while fulfilling daily obligations at the same time. These include needlework (collars), writing (letters), gardening (faucet handles and dried grasses), and cooking (utensils). These activities contributed to the welfare of the family, of course. But more importantly, in my view, they fed and continued to feed the artists."

Bohemian Room

In today's world, the word "Bohemian" means different things to different people. In popular usage, it often refers to non-traditional, counter-cultural people who dress colorfully and live a free-spirited existence, like the American artists and writers who settled in Paris during the 1920s. Some poets of the beat generation, who prepared the way for the culturally revolutionary 1960s, were known as Bohemians.

But there is a real place in the world called Bohemia. It is, along with Moravia and part of Silesia, one of three historic regions in the Czech Republic. Ironically, rather than being a society that eschews the traditional, Bohemia is a place of artistic tradition and culture — a culture that is connected with the culture of Iowa.

A beloved citizen of Bohemia, composer Antonin Dvorák, completed his great symphony "From The New World" in a small Iowan immigrant community called Spillville. Because of him, and because of those less well-known men, women, and children who came to the Midwest from his corner of Europe, the Bohemian Room was created in the Hotel Pattee.

The room reflects the folk art culture of Bohemia — an art form that is vividly colorful in design, rich in creativity and in handcraft motifs. Tracie McCloskey writes of the room, "One closet is a curio for Bohemian Glass and other indigenous artifacts such as an antique wedding bonnet embroidered with gold and garnets. Embroideries have been made into pillows, and a few are shadow-boxed with black and cream Czechoslovakian fabric. Large black embroidered ribbons accent the window seat cushion, and Czech lace softens the windows. We have a wonderful painted antique trunk elevated on legs to act as a table in front of the window seat."

In the early decades of the Nineteenth Century, painted furniture became the pride of Bohemian village households. Only certain objects were painted, usually those that a bride would bring as her dowry: china cupboards, beds, and chests and wardrobes. The painting style of Northeastern Bohemia, incorporating floral patterns and figures, is unique in Europe. Painter Judith Kjenstad, who also worked in the hotel's Dutch Room, has faithfully reproduced these colorful designs on the Bohemian Room's furniture.

Intricately painted eggs provide accents in the room. They, too, have an interesting history. "Kraslice (decorated eggs) are not a recent development," McCloskey continues. "They date back at least to the Fourteenth Century. Each district in Bohemia decorated eggs differently, and it is possible to recognize the difference in regions. Young women gave decorated eggs to young men at Easter, as a traditional symbol of new life and fertility."

The Bohemian Room is a tribute to a people. It also recalls the talent of Antonin Dvorák, who not only completed his "New World" Symphony in Iowa, but also completed sketches for his String Quartet in F, Opus 96, which is sometimes referred to as the Spillville Quartet. It is said that Dvorák wrote quickly and with great inspiration in Iowa, because he felt a spiritual connection to the countryside, which so closely resembled his Czech homeland.

Left: Detail from painted cabinet depicting St. Adalbert, the founder of the Benedict monastery in Prague. *Below:* Bohemian glass.

Italian Room

Along with Welsh, Bohemians, and other Europeans, Italians began to arrive in Iowa toward the end of the Nineteenth Century, and many of them found work for themselves in coal mining. Most immigrants from Italy arrived in the Midwest without agricultural skills, and so were attracted to other forms of employment. Often the men came alone, sponsored by relatives or friends already in America. After they had paid off their sponsors, they saved enough money to bring their wives and children from Italy. Two generations of Italians worked in Iowa's mining industry before the mines began to close in the 1920s.

Roberta Ahmanson recalls, "I went to school with the Fioris, who attended the Catholic Church. There were other people of Italian descent in Perry as well, so we wanted to remember them. Then there's a Des Moines woman, Amy Worthen, who spends part of every year in Venice. Three of her etchings are in the room, and they are really wonderful, evocative pieces." Also dis-played in the room are photographs of Perry's Fruit Market, which was owned by Frank Bordenaro, another local Italian American, during the mid-1900s. His daughter and granddaughter still live in Perry.

The Italian Room, like Amy Worthen's artwork, recalls an Italian villa. The walls have been aged; the drapery fabric is antique, dating to around 1910. Tracie McCloskey bought the Fortuny silk light fixture in Venice. The iron bed was custom-designed and made for the room, and the mirror and small console are antique pieces from the Eighteenth and Nineteenth Centuries. The room contains weavings from Assisi, too, as well as Carlo Moretti contemporary glass pieces.

Of the colorful border, Tracie recalls, "Roberta found a photograph in a book of a vintage painting with a border detail the size of my baby finger nail. We kept enlarging it and enlarging it to adapt it. It was such a complicated process but now it looks great. Once the photo mural was completed, that kind of determined the colors of the room for the fabrics and the rest of the decor."

A painting by David Kreitzer of the Trevi Fountain provides a splash of Roman romance to the room, just as an exquisite glass chandelier crowns the decor with elegance and grace. The chandelier is from Murano, a Venetian island, which has long been the home of some of the world's most beautiful glass.

Above left: Malioca ceramic plate.
Right: Murano glass champagne flute by Carlo Moretti. *Below:* Detail from tile depicting the Italian art of ceramics.

Japanese Room

"It's like walking into a different world," says a guest, transfixed by her surroundings, standing inside the Japanese Room for the first time. Certainly this room, designed by a descendant of Harvey Willis, the founder of Perry, is one of the most unexpected settings in the Hotel Pattee. Luke Yosuke Willis's mother is Japanese; his father, David Willis, is a schoolmate of Roberta Green Ahmanson. Luke is an architecture and fine arts graduate of the Rhode Island School of Design. He was commissioned to create a Japanese Room for the hotel, and the results are a taste of contemporary Japan.

Willis created a furnitureless room, where an elevated ground provides space for seating and sleeping, and minimal screens hide doors in order to maximize the area. There is no clutter, only the Japanese experience of sleeping and sitting, yet experienced in a comfortable way. It is a tranquil room, accented with a slate entry, bamboo flooring, *tatami* mats, and a futon-style bed. Comple-

menting Luke Willis's work are light sofits, wood paneling, a *tansu* cabinet and shelves, screens, *shoji* panels, and a bamboo niche, built by Chadwick and Bergstrom furniture in Des Moines. Eric Pereza constructed the desk and benches, the platform for the *tatami* mats, and the *tansu* chest in the entry.

"The selection of the vertical grain Douglas fir, with its long, even grain, worked perfectly with the subtle and simple forms that the Japanese style represents," writes Brian Bergstrom. "All the lumber for the project was shipped from Washington State to our shop in Des Moines….Twelve-foot lengths were necessary to minimize the number of vertical joints on the horizontal panels, and especially the cabinets that house the *tansu* drawer section and shelves. This was assembled on site and installed as one cabinet. The screens and *shoji* panels, made of handmade paper from Thailand, were the biggest challenge of engineering and construction."

Isamu Noguchi's *akari* lamp provides subtle lighting. The Japanese word for light also carries the implications of weightlessness. Noguchi combines light and the illusion of weightlessness in his lamps. Although delicate in appearance, they are strong. The *washi* paper of which they are handcrafted is made from mulberry tree bark, which is shaped on a *higo* bamboo ribbing frame.

Against the tranquil backdrop created by these gifted designers are two fine paintings by renowned artist Makoto Fujimura. Using a medieval Japanese technique called *nihonga*, which entails the layering of mineral pigments, he has applied gold, silver, and crushed precious

minerals on *kumohada* paper. Of these two paintings, "Golden Forest" and "Gravity and Grace," the artist says, "The painting materials reflect my respect for traditional Japanese work, but also my interest in the contemporary, process-oriented dialogue developing in New York City where I work and live."

"Golden Forest" is one of Fujimura's series of paintings of pine forests. Another major work from this series called "Golden Pine" now hangs in the atrium of the AOL/Time Warner Building in Hong Kong. "Gravity and Grace" is painted with pure mineral pigment colors. The artist says, "As calligraphers of

Above left: Detail from *Golden Forest* by Makoto Fujimura. *Below:* Detail of bamboo arrangement.

the ancient world captured and distilled ideas and experiences in simple strokes, these paintings use expressionistic movement and use of gravity, allowing the pigment to cascade down. The resulting semi-opaque surface traps refractive light, creating what I call a 'grace arena,' an optical effect that only the naked eye can capture. I based this painting upon the experience of seeing tree swallows of Vail, Colorado, sweeping through the crisp morning air, creating calligraphy in the azurite sky.

"A research scientist friend once told me that the autumn leaves are most beautiful on the trees by the roadside because they happen to be distressed by the salt and pollution. Every sunset is a reminder of the impending death of Nature herself. The minerals I use must be pulverized to bring out their beauty. The Japanese were right in associating beauty with death. Art cannot be divorced from faith, for to do so is to literally close our eyes to that beauty of the dying sun setting all around us. Every beauty suffers. Death spreads all over our lives and therefore faith must be given to see through the darkness, to see through the beauty of 'the valley of the shadow of death.'"

Left: Japanese Room with painting (Makoto Fujimura, *Golden Forest*).

Makoto Fujimura
New York, New York

Born in Boston in 1960, Makoto Fujimura was educated both in the United States and in Japan, where he began to consider the possibility of combining American abstract expressionism with aspects of a traditional Japanese art form called Nihonga. Fujimura spent six and a half years learning the Nihonga technique, in which materials such as malachite, azurite, and other minerals are mixed with animal skin glue and applied to special paper. Today, because of his artistic prestige in both the United States and Japan, Fujimura has become a voice of bicultural authority on the nature and cultural assessment of beauty, by both creating it and exploring its forms.

Currently he is serving as a member of the National Council on the Arts, the advisory body of the National Endowment for the Arts.

Luke Willis
Providence, Rhode Island

Luke Willis, whose personal history bridges Iowa's culture and Japan's, describes the idea behind his work, "Quite contrary to the vast spaces available in Iowa, Japan has experienced a shortage of space for centuries. As a result, the Japanese developed a poetic usage of space in order to intensify certain qualities within a given area. The traditional Japanese room simulates interior space to continue visual movement and feelings into the exterior, beyond the actual physical thresholds, thereby maximizing spatial feelings. We can see this as revealing high respect and concern for the environment in Japan, since the exterior environment is no longer separate from the world one lives in inside a house or room. I believe that there are similar values and connections which people hold for the vast landscape of Iowa, where the immediate ties to landscape exist in daily lives as well."

Angus and Moran Room

Along with its ethnic and cultural variety, Iowa's agricultural tradition is central to its identity. Popular images of Iowa usually include rolling waves of cornstalks, soybean fields, and well-kept farmhouses. It is difficult, therefore, to imagine that by 1867, when the Northwestern Railroad reached Council Bluffs, Iowa was the leading coal producer west of the Mississippi River, and fifth in coal production in America. Angus, Iowa, the town that was one of the most prosperous of all the Iowa mining communities, is located just five miles north of Perry.

Coal was discovered in 1866 and the first shaft mine was sunk on Snake Creek in 1868. Angus began as Coaltown in 1869 and was renamed and incorporated as Angus in 1883. It was the largest coal-mining town in Iowa in 1885, with a population of about 5,000. After a general miners' strike in late 1884 and an ensuing riot, the town began its rapid decline. By 1900 the population of Angus was about 333. The last mine closed in 1930.

Moran, another mining center, is about twelve miles southeast of Perry.

In 1917, the first mineshaft was dug on the Billy Moran farm. An underground lake was struck, and little progress was made. Then Norwood-White Coal Company bought the rights, sealed the water from the shaft, and successfully mined there until 1940, when a fire closed the Moran mine.

There is more reason than geographical proximity for Perry to remember Angus — some historians estimate that literally hundreds of residences in Perry have been reconstructed out of buildings moved from Angus when the mining industry collapsed in the early years of the Twentieth Century. Once the mines began to close, Angus — which once held the promise of being one of Iowa's most thriving communities — and Moran shuttered their shops and were quickly transformed into near ghost towns.

But before their rather abrupt closing, the mines employed workers from myriad backgrounds. Some of the mineworkers were African Americans. Others were new arrivals from the old country. After the mines began to close, some immigrant miners — from Cornwall, England; Wales; Italy; Bohemia; and Eastern Europe — stayed in Iowa, found new means of livelihood, and became a permanent part of Iowa's ethnic tapestry. The Angus and Moran Room at the Hotel Pattee was created to honor Iowa's miners and the towns they built with their hard-earned coal dollars.

The room was designed to be similar to a coal miner's home — cottage style, like the Irish and Welsh rooms. Tracie McCloskey says, "They lived simply, and so this room is pretty simple. We used quilts and tweed fabrics as well as plain, practical furniture and authentic artifacts."

The Angus and Moran Room frieze is made up of actual photographs of the mines and of the two communities "then and now." There's a canary in a birdcage in the room, which has been made into a lamp, recalling the grim threat of toxic gasses underground. A canary was carried into a mine, and if it died, the miners knew that they should flee or deadly fumes would kill them, too. Another lamp is made of a miner's hat. The fabrics in the room are all tweeds of working-class style. Displayed prominently in the room is a Betty Lenz quilt, commemorating the Angus and Moran mines and miners.

Describing the quilt, the award-winning quilt maker says, "I chose to use the block pattern 'Dutchman's Puzzle' to represent the immigrants and also to represent the huge fans used to ventilate the underground tunnels. I found it fascinating that mules were used underground to pull the loaded cars to the lift. I listed a number of the larger, more active mines in the surrounding border. There are two photos, transferred to cloth in the quilt. The lower photo is assumed to have been taken in the late 1800s; the other, with more advanced equipment, was possibly taken in the 1920s or 1930s."

Above left: Quilt by Betty Lenz featuring Dutchman's Puzzle design.

Dutch Room

On the frieze of the Dutch Room, the saying goes, *Wie verre reizen doet kan veel verhalen*. In English, that means, "Those who travel far can tell many stories." Surely one of the most important stories well-informed travelers can tell about Iowa is the story of the Dutch settlers, who came to America from the Netherlands in search of farmland and a place to live their faith. Like the Germans, the Dutch arrived with their families, and they formed their own communities, which revolved around their Reformed churches.

The Dutch were a visible presence in the state by 1870, when one-tenth of all the foreign-born Dutch in America lived in Iowa (4,513). The founder of Pella, Iowa, Hendrick Pieter Scholte, is said to be the person most responsible for establishing a tight-knit Iowa Dutch population. Although he and others had once considered settling in Holland, Michigan, Scholte concluded it was too far north, and its forests were incompatible with the Dutch people's agricultural interests. So Pella was founded in South Central Iowa in 1847 by some 800 Dutch immigrants. Later on, another community, Orange City, was settled in the northwestern part of the state.

The Dutch Room at the Hotel Pattee is dedicated to The Netherlands' Midwestern immigrants, and the artwork in the room reflects both their European roots and their Christian faith. Perhaps one of the most dramatic rooms in the hotel, the Dutch Room features a built-in Dutch-style bed and a hand carved Dutch oak fireplace dating from 1837. The room is decorated in the Hindeloopen style, a Dutch folk art tradition that features woodcarving and colorful painted surfaces.

Else Bigton and Phillip Odden, who constructed the room's furniture, sought to "make this room come alive with a pleasant blending of strong furniture forms, colorful organic ornamentation, and familiar Biblical scenes." Bigton and Odden have become well known for their carving of the curls and scrolls of the acanthus leaf motif and the intertwining dragons, serpents, and leafage that are typical of the carving found in Norway's ornate medieval stave churches.

Judith Kjenstad, who did the painting in the room, was commissioned to depict Biblical scenes, which are common themes in Dutch folk painting. In the Dutch Room are images taken from the story of Creation in the Book of Genesis, including the casting out of Adam and Eve from the Garden of Eden. Other images include Moses parting the Red Sea, Noah's flood, and the Patriarch Abraham and his wife Sarah extending hospitality to three angels. Of her work at the Hotel Pattee, Ms. Kjenstad says, "The biggest compliment you can give artists is to allow them to do their work. That is the opportunity I was given in decorating the Dutch Room."

The Hindeloopen style of the Dutch Room is complemented by the fabric used in the bedding and upholstery, all of which came from Hindeloopen, in the north of The Netherlands. Also featured in the room is the work of Dutch American artist Elinor Noteboom, who lives in Orange City, Iowa.

".... My own roots are deep
in the dark soil of northwest Iowa
and Orange City where every
year we celebrate the Tulip Festival
with authentic costumes, food,
dances, performances, and parades.
This festival shows up in some
of my prints and paintings.
These are always full of celebration."
— Elinor Noteboom

Meanwhile, the sayings on the frieze of the Dutch Room deserve thought and consideration. They were compiled by the Rev. Cornelius Plantinga, Jr., who is president of Calvin Theological Seminary, where men and women are trained to serve in Reformed churches. One of the quotes says, *Van het concert des levens*

Above left: Detail of Delft tile.

Judy Kjenstad
Minneapolis, Minnesota

Judith Nelson Kjenstad has studied and worked with decorative painting for more than twenty-four years. She began with Norwegian rosemaling, studying with the Norwegian masters at the Norwegian American Museum in Decorah, Iowa. This led to a Gold Medal in rosemaling and finally, to a degree in design from the University of Minnesota. Commissions and teaching assignments in rosemaling, Swedish painting, florals, and other types of large-scale work have taken her across the country from Epcot® in Florida to Seattle and Chicago.

Of her work painting the Biblical scenes for the Dutch Room in the Hotel Pattee, Kjenstad writes, "The base-coating of the large case pieces was somewhat exhausting, but the chance to paint on this great furniture built by Else Bigton and Phillip Odden was, as always, a real treat. I was also fortunate to be able to work (for the first time) with my daughter. It was a bit like painting with another me — a little spooky and very satisfying."

krijgt niemand een programma. In English, that simply means, "No gets a program for the concert of life."

Perhaps there is no program, but one thing is clear: the concert of life in America's Midwest would not be complete without the contributions of the Dutch. Their gifts to the community of strong character, artistic accomplishment, and solid faith are evident in their culture—then and now.

Left: Detail of hand painted, built-in bed with painting (Judith Kjenstad, *Angels Visit to Patriarch Abraham*). *Above:* Detail of cabinets hand painted by Judith Kjenstad featuring scenes from the Biblical creation story.

Welsh Room

When our world lies dark in sadness. Every star shines down its gladness.
O mor siriol gwêna seren. I oleuo'i chwaer-ddaearen. Ar hy

The stories that recount the struggle of immigrants attempting to relocate in the United States are often poignant. "My grandfather came from Wales when he was fourteen in 1914," Pam Jenkins says, "And he came by himself on the ship. He actually ended up in Minnesota and then settled outside of Perry on a farm. Like him, the Welsh, although they were farmers, often came to the Midwest as did the Czechoslovakians and others, as laborers. And so you don't see as strong a component of the Welsh in Iowa as you do the other major immigrant groups. But they brought with them their own traditions."

The Welsh also brought to America their love for music — especially singing — as well as poetry, drama, and art. And they brought their strong religious faith. There is a saying among the Welsh, "The first thing a Frenchman does in a new country is to build a trading post, an American builds a city, a German builds a beer hall, and a Welshman builds a church."

The Welsh Room in the Hotel Pattee is decorated in the style of a Welsh cottage. It is furnished in tweeds, and it contains an exquisite quilt miniature entitled "A Visit to Wales II," which was especially made for the room by Wisconsin quilter Diane Gaudynski. She writes, "Inspired by the vintage quilts of Wales, this miniature uses many quilting motifs found in large whole-cloth Welsh and English quilts as well as my own feathers and urns on the outer border." With a reputation for the use of dull "mud" colors, Ms. Gaudynski specializes in ornate, intricate machine quilting of traditional and original feather designs.

The room is accessorized with items beloved by the Welsh people — including antique "Gaudy" china pieces and a collection of books, including the poetry of Welsh poet Dylan Thomas. And to commemorate the tradition of Welsh mines and miners, whose industry has played such an essential role in Wales' economy (for good reason, the Welsh room connects with the Angus and Moran Room), there is a lamp fashioned of a brass coal miner's lamp. As a tribute to Pam Jenkins' grandfather and his courageous journey from Wales, the Welsh Room wing chair and ottoman are covered in the Jenkins of Wales Tartan, which was also used for the bed skirts.

Jen Jones, whose popular shop in Ceredigion, Wales, specializes in antique Welsh textiles, provided some unique items from the late Nineteenth Century for the room's decor. A pillow is fashioned from two antique Welsh skirts; three pillow shams are made of antique

Welsh blankets; and another similar blanket, but boldly striped, is folded at the foot of the bed.

The curtains in the Welsh room are designed from fabric with a unique traditional Welsh weave. This fabric is manufactured at the Trefriw Woolen Mills, which have been situated on the banks of the River Crafnant in Wales for more than 100 years. In the process of manufacturing woolens, the Trefriw

Above left: Welsh love spoons. *Above right:* Detail of the Welsh National Anthem, *Hen Wlad Fy Nhadau,* calligraphy and illumination by Darren Evans.

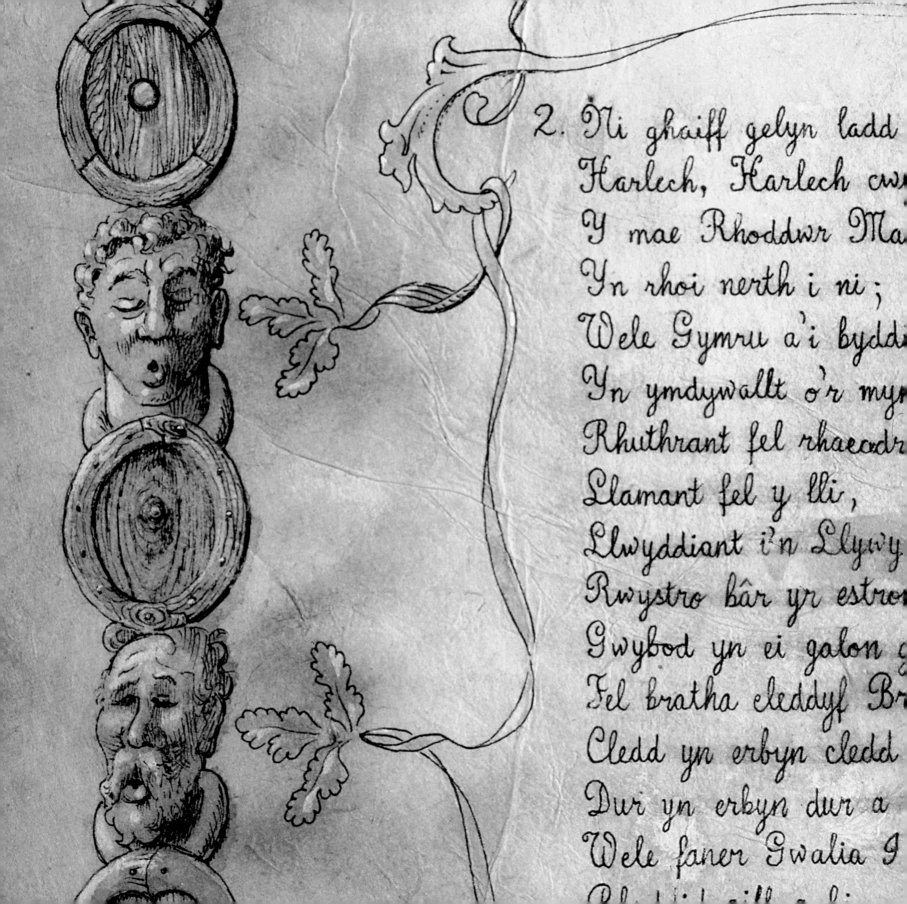

2. Ni ghaiff gelyn ladd
Harlech, Harlech cw
Y mae Rhoddwr Ma
Yn rhoi nerth i ni;
Wele Gymru a'i bydd
Yn ymdywallt o'r myn
Rhuthrant fel rhaeadr
Llamant fel y lli,
Llwyddiant i'n Llywy
Rwystro bâr yr estron
Gwybod yn ei galon g
Fel bratha cleddyf Br
Cledd yn erbyn cledd
Dur yn erbyn dur a
Wele faner Gwalia I

Mills do virtually everything but shear the sheep. They blend together the raw wool, card it, spin it, double it, dye it, warp it, and finally weave it into richly textured and colored fabrics.

Prominently displayed in the room are Welsh love spoons, as they are often called. Hand carved of wood with great care and detail, they represent an old courtship tradition in Wales. Once upon a time, a young man carved just such a spoon for the girl of his dreams. He knew that the more intricate and beautiful the design, the better his chances were to win the heart of his ladylove.

Nervous and hopeful, the suitor offered his spoon to the young woman. If she returned it, the young man's heart was broken — at least for a while. But if she chose to keep the spoon, her willingness to accept it promised the pair a happy future.

Love spoons continue to be symbols of Welsh culture today and are cherished treasures for souvenir collectors in Wales.

Alongside these memorabilia of Welsh heritage, perhaps the most representative feature of the Welsh Room is the custom calligraphy of two Welsh songs in the room's entryway. They were fashioned by Darren Evans, presently of Des Moines, who was born in Tenby, Wales, a small town on the southwest coast in the county of Pembrokeshire. He calls his art company "Wilddoodle," and his work appears in several other Hotel Pattee guest rooms.

Of the Welsh Room paintings Evans says, "Having grown up in Wales and with a rich musical background, I was very enthusiastic about creating these aged musical scripts. The famous march, 'The Men of Harlech,' celebrates the defiance of the Welsh forces in defending Harlech Castle against the English in 1468. I imagined these guys singing their hearts out, as Welsh folk do, as they kept watch from the castle walls."

O'er the hills though night lies sleeping,
Tongues of flame through mists
are leaping,
As the brave, their vigil keeping,
Front the deadly fray.
Then the battle thunder,
tears the rocks asunder,
As the light falls on the flight of foes
without their plunder;
There the vanquished horde is routed,
There the valiant never doubted,
There they died but dying shouted
"Freedom wins the day."

The other song painted on the Welsh Room walls by Wilddoodle is "Hen Wlad Fy Nhadau," the Welsh National Anthem. Evans says, "I've known it in my pidgin Welsh for as long as I can remember. I incorporated this song into a setting that represents everything of Wales to me — the Pembrokeshire coastline — the perfect backdrop for a song. If you ever have the opportunity to sing with a large crowd of Welsh folk, then you'll probably declare yourself Welsh. And if you can sing with an ounce of passion, then you probably are!"

Left: Detail of *The Men of Harlach* by Darren Evans. *Next page:* Detail of Hotel Pattee spa, lower level.

Darren Evans
Des Moines

Wilddoodle's Darren Evans has a biography and artistic history as colorful and varied as his artwork. He attended art college for five years in Carmarthen, Wales, as well as in Falmouth and Plymouth, England, and in Des Moines, Iowa. He has supported himself through many art mediums— he has installed wood floors, worked in graphic design, created computer graphics, animated films, (Walt Disney's Who Framed Roger Rabbit*), and has designed everything from books to signs to tattoos. Darren has "…painted signs on the Greek island of Rhodes and worked as a portrait artist on the streets of London and Minneapolis." He contributed to the Living History Farms in Iowa by producing for them both illustrations and maps. He has gained invaluable experience in restoration by working for three years with EverGreene Painting Studios of New York. Another restoration project of his was to help strip and regild the Iowa State Capitol dome.*

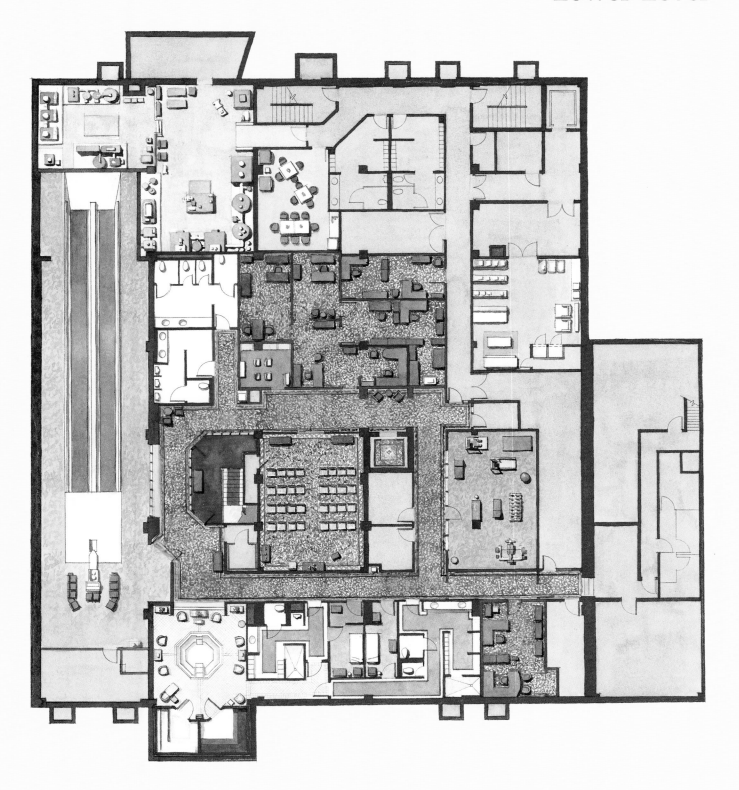

Arthur "Oley" Olson Bowling Alley

As you've seen by now, every room in the Hotel Pattee has a story to tell. Take, for example, the Arthur "Oley" Olson Bowling Alley located on the Lower Level. Clearly, there are few fine hotels in the world whose guests are able to enjoy a bowling alley all their own. Why a bowling alley? Because it replicates one that was located in approximately the same place when the hotel was new.

The winter of 1936 was a terrible one. Ned Willis once noted, "They closed the school for, I think, a whole week. Everything was shut down. So the hotel said if you set your own pins, you can come down and bowl for free."

Roberta Ahmanson recalls, "When my grandfather stayed in the hotel in 1932, before the family could move up from Des Moines, he bowled there. He often took one of his kids along on weekends, and my mother remembers bowling there with him."

Mrs. Ahmanson continues, "My grandfather's name was Arthur Oscar Olson, but everybody called him Oley.

He was born in 1890 in Clive, Iowa, which is part of Des Moines now. He started as a telegrapher on the railroad when he was nine years old, and he was still a railroad telegrapher when he came to Perry as the Chief Night Dispatcher. One of the pictures in the bowling alley is of him sitting at his desk during his dispatching job. There's also a newspaper photograph of him with his bowling team, holding a bowling ball. And then there's the item from 1926 when he was second in the American Bowling Congress Championships. It was in Ohio, and I think he won fifty dollars."

The original bowling alley was eventually torn out of the Hotel Pattee, but a new version of it was installed during the remodel. And, of course, it was named after Roberta Green Ahmanson's grandfather — the Arthur "Oley" Olson Bowling Alley — because, to this day, he remains Perry's most famous bowler.

Oley Olson was also a great friend to local athletes. Because of his avid interest in sports, one wall of the bowling alley is filled with Perry sports photographs. These include Bob Feller, Dallas County's most famous baseball player; and a picture of Babe Ruth, who visited Perry in the 1920s and lunched in the Hotel. Also displayed are enlargements of 1915 advertisements for Perry businesses and an oil painting called "The Bowler," by Iowa artist John Vander Stelt.

Mr. and Mrs. Howard Cox, who once owned Perry Bowl, presented a unique gift to the Oley Olson Bowling Alley. They donated two special bowling balls, which were drilled with various size finger holes and spans between the thumb and finger holes. The balls were used for sizing; the measurements they provided made it possible to custom drill bowling balls for individual customers.

Above left: Bill Whiton, Clyde Kirkman, Art Olson, Howard Cox, Warren Hoyt, c. 1956. *Below:* Detail of the Arthur "Oley" Olsen Bowling Alley.

Nicollet Room

Like the Canisteo Room on the First Floor, the Nicollet Room is a popular hotel gathering place, named for a type of rich Midwestern soil. Found both in Minnesota and in Iowa, Nicollet is one of the fertile farming soils that surround Perry, Iowa. A soil core sample is displayed in the room, provided by Iowa State University.

The room also contains the handwork of two well-known American quilters, whose work is also displayed elsewhere in the Hotel Pattee.

Betty Lenz's award-winning quilts are based on traditional patterns, but are contemporary in design. In her creative process, she uses appliqué, embroidery, and beading, as well as quilt patterns such as the corn-and-beans pattern, which is the basis for "Behold All That Is Iowa," the quilt in the Nicollet Room. In its design, artist Lenz incorporated the wild rose, which is the Iowa state flower, and the live oak, the state tree.

On the opposite wall is a quilt by Murray Johnston, a contemporary folk art quilt maker who lives in Alabama. Roberta Ahmanson first met her in 1990 in Ashville, North Carolina, at a craft fair.

"I own several of her quilts," Mrs. Ahmanson says. "When my dad died, my mother and I had all his shirts and were wondering what to do with them. I wrote to Murray and asked her if she would make a quilt out of them. I sent her the eulogy and obituary and the shirts, and what she made as a result was very moving. For the Nicollet

Room, she did a contemporary quilt that's called 'All That is Perry,' with buildings from Perry and the railroad track. She actually printed a grid map of the town on some fabric, and that fabric is part of the quilt."

The Nicollet Room, which is used for a wide variety of small local events like showers, anniversaries, birthdays, and similar functions, exhibits a collection of drawings that were made by young Perry students who competed in art contests during the hotel's re-

opening. Also featured is a print by American artist Betye Saar honoring her parents — an African American man married to an Irish woman. Iowa, with its multi-cultural heritage, was one of the few states in America where such interracial marriage was permitted in the early Twentieth Century.

Left: Murray Johnston, Quilt, *All That is Perry,* 2000. *Above:* Betty Lenz, Quilt, *Behold All That Is Iowa, 1997.*

Harve Siglin Boiler Room

In 1947, Siglin Plumbing and Heating Company in Perry installed the boiler for the newly refurbished Hotel Pattee. When the hotel was being renovated in 1997 and workers were putting in a new heating and cooling system and new boiler, Harve Siglin showed up at the hotel to see it. "I bet yours won't last as long as mine did," he said.

"So," Roberta Ahmanson explains, "I decided that we should name the boiler room after him, and it is indeed, the Harve Siglin Boiler Room. There's a picture and an article about Harve beside the door."

Nell Quinlisk Staff Lounge

Directly across from the boiler room is the Nell Quinlisk Staff Lounge, named for a woman who served the Hotel Pattee as a waitress for many years. The lounge is furnished with Arts and Crafts furniture and is decorated with David

Kreitzer paintings. Roberta Ahmanson remembers Nell Quinlisk.

"She was the kind of waitress that told you what you were going to have and how much you were going to like it. You didn't really have to worry much about ordering because she was perfectly happy to do that for you. She was kind of gruff, but everybody loved her. And the legend is that she could carry nine plates on her arms. I thought she should be remembered."

Josephine Lee Laundry

Josephine Lee worked in the Hotel Pattee's laundry room during the 1950s. During those years Louis Armstrong stayed in the hotel (see Louis Armstrong Suite, page 96). When the great jazz trumpet player performed, he perspired heavily and frequently mopped his face with a handkerchief. He also used handkerchiefs to wipe his mouth after blowing the trumpet. Clearly, "Satchmo" needed a large number of clean handkerchiefs on hand, and he sent twenty-five handkerchiefs to the hotel laundry. He liked to pull them out of his pocket with a dramatic flair, and so he wanted them folded a certain way. He included a note, explaining exactly how he wanted the folds done.

Josephine Lee dutifully laundered the handkerchiefs, and she and the women who worked with her tried their best to fold the handkerchiefs according to Armstrong's instructions. Unfortunately, they just couldn't get it right. Josephine, who had plenty of other laundry to do, became somewhat exasperated with the whole assignment.

So she ironed the handkerchiefs flat, turned Armstrong's note over and wrote on the back, "Fold them yourself."

Josephine Lee is now in her 90s and still recalls the incident with pride and humor. Pam Jenkins says, "When you talk to her, she has the best sense of humor. You hear her life story. She has a unique kind of spirit about her life and about the many years she worked. The Josephine Lee Laundry honors the hard-working people of the Perry community."

Left: Harve Siglin, 2003. *Below left:* Nell Quinlisk Staff Lounge with paintings by David Kreitzer. *Above:* Josephine Lee, 2003.

Acknowledgements

Bill Clark
Vice-President, Pattee Enterprises;
Vice-Chair, Hotel Pattee;
President, Hometown Perry, Iowa

Bill Clark has been deeply involved in with projects in Perry, Iowa, since 1993, when the Hotel Pattee went on the auction block. A longtime friend of Roberta Ahmanson, he was asked to bid on it on behalf of Pattee Enterprises. He subsequently oversaw its demolition and has since been responsible for supervising virtually every aspect of its renovation. Clark recalls innumerable mishaps with flooding, electrical crises, untimely deliveries, and moments of great delight and success during the long journey to the Hotel Pattee's completed renovation. "While it has nearly killed me at times," he recalls, "it has also exposed me to some incredible talent and wonderful people."

Rhonda Volz
Project Manager

With a background in creative projects and interior design application, Rhonda Volz oversees construction and remodeling at the Hotel Pattee, as well as for Pattee Enterprises and Hometown Perry, Iowa. Starting with the creative vision of Roberta Ahmanson and working with Bill Clark, Volz is responsible for timely implementation of multiple tasks, including coordination with contractors, designers, and the hotel manager. "I now oversee construction on all of the Pattee Enterprises projects as well as any changes made in the hotel. I especially enjoyed managing the Inter-Urban Lounge project," Rhonda Volz says. "It turned out beautifully. I thrive on a full plate, and this job gives me just that."

Ann Hirou
Project Manager

Ann Hirou worked in advertising and marketing until she was hired by the Ahmansons in 1995. She says, "Because my primary position on the Ahmansons' California staff is to manage their art collection, it has been my great pleasure to work with that portion of the collection residing at the Hotel Pattee. My involvement with the hotel has expanded my world in so many ways. I have been exposed to a wide variety of extraordinary people: artists, craftsmen, designers, and thinkers. And I have worked with people of great vision and talent and dedication." Since the hotel's grand re-opening in 1997, Ann Hirou has been involved in a number of projects from developing the Ray B. Smith Museum Store, which serves as the hotel's gift shop, to decorating the hotel for Christmas. She also serves as project manager for Hotel Pattee book projects, which have included *Lit by the Sun* and *Inside the Hotel Pattee.*

Tracie McCloskey
Interior Designer

After thirty years of owning her own design firm, where she specialized in residential design, Tracie McCloskey moved into commercial and professional projects as her clientele grew. After the Hotel Pattee opened, Pattee Enterprises hired her "to take the rooms at the Hotel Pattee a few steps further, which was a great experience." Describing her work at the Hotel Pattee, McCloskey says, "I am often asked, what is my favorite room — a very difficult question that seems to change on each visit. But I do know that my favorite thing to do while visiting is to observe guests as they experience the hotel and its rooms. Like me, they are constantly amazed at the beautiful attention to quality and detail. This project has been an experience I treasure. I look forward to seeing the awareness of the art and history that the hotel and its future projects will present to Perry — a small town with a big heart."

Pam Jenkins
Research Director at Hometown Perry, Iowa.

Pam Jenkins, a sociologist who studies communities, grew up in Perry, Iowa, and is now a professor at the University of New Orleans. "My work in Perry has been some of the most rewarding of my career," Jenkins says. "I believe that the Hotel Pattee reflects an understanding of how communities work together. Moreover, several of the rooms have personal meaning for me and they illustrate the heritage of my own family's work and labor." For Jenkins, the daughter of a railroader, the public spaces that document the railroads' influence in Perry are important. "As someone who grew up in Perry, the rooms tell the story of a Midwestern small-town life. For example, the Cream 'n' Eggs Room honors farmwomen, including my grandmother and aunts, who helped provide income for their farm families. Also, the Alton School Room connects me to the long tradition of teachers, now five generations, in my family."

John Leusink
Architect

John Leusink's architectural firm, Wetherell, Ericsson, Leusink Architects, is located in Des Moines, Iowa. He is in his eighth year of working with Pattee Enterprises on various projects throughout Perry. His most recent project was the completion of the Inter-Urban Lounge, in honor of Frank Lloyd Wright. "Over the course of these years, Mrs. Ahmanson's vision has never wavered," he says. "Every design decision is carefully considered. Every detail is deliberated. Every visual element is examined. All this exhaustive study is done to assure each environment speaks of honesty, integrity, and delight."

Index